real life
decorating

Better Homes and Gardens® Books · Des Moines, Iowa

BETTER HOMES AND GARDENS® BOOKS,
AN IMPRINT OF MEREDITH® BOOKS

real life decorating

EDITOR: LINDA HALLAM
SENIOR ASSOCIATE DESIGN DIRECTOR: RICHARD MICHELS
CONTRIBUTING PHOTOGRAPHERS: GORDON BEALL,
  D.RANDOLPH FOULDS, SUSAN GILMORE, BILL HOLT,
  JENIFER JORDAN, EMILY MINTON
COPY CHIEF: CATHERINE HAMRICK
COPY AND PRODUCTION EDITOR: TERRI FREDRICKSON
BOOK PRODUCTION MANAGERS: PAM KVITNE,
  MARJORIE J. SCHENKELBERG
CONTRIBUTING COPY EDITOR: CAROL BOKER
CONTRIBUTING PROOFREADERS: SUSAN J. KLING, DAN DEGEN,
  MARGARET SMITH
INDEXER: KATHLEEN POOLE
ELECTRONIC PRODUCTION COORDINATOR: PAULA FOREST
EDITORIAL AND DESIGN ASSISTANTS: KAYE CHABOT,
  MARY LEE GAVIN, KAREN SCHIRM

MEREDITH® BOOKS
EDITOR IN CHIEF: JAMES D. BLUME
DESIGN DIRECTOR: MATT STRELECKI
MANAGING EDITOR: GREGORY H. KAYKO
EXECUTIVE SHELTER EDITOR: DENISE L. CARINGER

DIRECTOR, RETAIL SALES AND MARKETING: TERRY UNSWORTH
DIRECTOR, SALES, SPECIAL MARKETS: RITA MCMULLEN
DIRECTOR, SALES, PREMIUMS: MICHAEL A. PETERSON
DIRECTOR, SALES, RETAIL: TOM WIERZBICKI
DIRECTOR, SALES, HOME & GARDEN CENTERS: RAY WOLF
DIRECTOR, BOOK MARKETING: BRAD ELMITT
DIRECTOR, OPERATIONS: GEORGE A. SUSRAL
DIRECTOR, PRODUCTION: DOUGLAS M. JOHNSTON

VICE PRESIDENT, GENERAL MANAGER: JAMIE L. MARTIN

BETTER HOMES AND GARDENS® MAGAZINE
EDITOR IN CHIEF: JEAN LEMMON
EXECUTIVE INTERIOR DESIGN EDITOR: SANDRA S. SORIA

MEREDITH PUBLISHING GROUP
PRESIDENT, PUBLISHING GROUP: CHRISTOPHER M. LITTLE
VICE PRESIDENT, FINANCE & ADMINISTRATION: MAX RUNCIMAN

MEREDITH CORPORATION
CHAIRMAN AND CHIEF EXECUTIVE OFFICER: WILLIAM T. KERR
CHAIRMAN OF THE EXECUTIVE COMMITTEE: E. T. MEREDITH III

All of us at Better Homes and
Gardens® Books are
dedicated to providing you
with information and ideas to
enhance your home. We
welcome your comments and
suggestions. Write to us at:
Better Homes and Gardens
Books, Shelter Editorial
Department, 1716 Locust St.,
Des Moines, IA 50309-3023.

If you would like to purchase
any of our books, check
wherever quality books are
sold. Visit our website at
bhg.com.

table of contents

what is

real life decorating?

your life, your style, your home

BY LINDA HALLAM / *REAL LIFE DECORATING* EDITOR

Real Life Decorating is decorating for how you live right now—for your lifestyle and life stage. That means enjoying your home today wherever you live and whatever your style and budget. It's finding your own starting point—a rug, collection, fabric, art, or paint color—to create your style and your home. And it means evolving the look of your home as your life changes.

My own decorating has been enriched by talented individuals who find joy and satisfaction in creating inviting personal spaces. In this book, you'll meet people who successfully decorate their homes to suit their circumstances and budgets. Their locations, occupations, lifestyles, and tastes differ, but they all possess a passion for good design and the tenacity to achieve it. These decorating enthusiasts generously share their tried-and-true advice, decorating lessons, affordable shopping resources, and other secrets throughout the book.

My real life decorating story began 15 years ago as I was rocking my youngest son in the living room of our small late-1940s house. I was thinking

about what color to paint the institutional green walls when a poster with shades of pink, a color we had never considered, caught my eye. In the months that followed, my husband Steve and I painted the living and dining areas pink and had washable white slipcovers made for our floral sofa and chair.

Later, for the same living room, we bought a 1930s Scottish wardrobe to store our television and compact disc player. The wardrobe was $250 at a thrift store. And we found a flat-woven kilim rug—navy and burgundy-red with all-important pink accents. The wardrobe, slipcovered furniture, and rug eventually moved with us across town to a larger, mid-1950s ranch-style house. We painted the living and dining rooms pale terra-cotta. I anchored the seating area with the kilim rug and the dining area with the wardrobe. Steve converted the wardrobe into our china cabinet. And I found an iron chandelier to hang over our Italian tile-and-pine dining table from an import store.

Life kept changing for us. Though we liked the house and loved the hilly

> **“** i'd rather buy art than a piece of furniture or a silver thing. buy art for yourself to make you happy. **”**
>
> CAMILO AND AURORA BARCENAS

> **“** this is a house for us right now, for children and terriers. we're saving the fancy stuff for later. **”**
>
> BILLY, DOROTHY, AND WILLIAM BOGER

neighborhood, we moved again—this time almost halfway across the country. The year we bought our present house was the same time our oldest son started college, a period of minimal money for decorating. We knew we couldn't buy anything major for the house. In the small living room with oak woodwork and a stone fireplace, the kilim rug works by balancing its color with rich red walls. The room is cozy for the cost of two gallons of paint. The wardrobe, too big for our small dining room, has found a new home. It houses the compact disc player, our china and silver, and bar supplies in the living room.

The living room also serves as the repository for my current collecting passion for brown-and-cream transferware pottery, family photographs, Steve's ship models, and dog figurines a friend brings us every summer from England.

Adjacent to the living room, our small dining room has one of my newer favorites—an old oval mirror in a distressed frame that I found while working on this book in Upstate New York. I struggled—literally—on planes, trains,

❝
our main
mantra for
this house:
when
you are
doing your
first house,
invest
money in
things you
can take
with you.
❞

SHELBY AND EVAN
SCHNEIDER

and taxis—to get this $60 secondhand-store find home. The chandelier and blue-and-white draperies, from the bedroom of our previous house, are in this cheerful yellow room. Last year, after I worked with a Boston designer, I emulated his idea of hanging blue-and-white plates with botanical prints.

For me, real life decorating evolves as my family moves and our sons grow up. Steve and I keep the furniture and accessories that work or that we can't afford to change. We add or subtract others as our space and budget allow—and our interests change. And one final personal note: I still have the poster that started my decorating. It no longer works in the living room, but it graces the hall outside our study/television room and reminds me of a dear friend.

The most interesting rooms and homes are never really finished. They continue to change and evolve over time, just as the people who live in them do. That's the joy and challenge of real life—and *Real Life Decorating*.

Linda Hallam / Editor of Real Life Decorating

❝
we don't
collect for
investment;
we collect
because we
love it. chips
don't bother
me; signs of
age make
things more
interesting.
❞

CAROLYN AND TOM
CARROLL

This book could not have been created without the partnership of talented art director Richard Michels. Rich and I worked together to find the 10 very different homes from across the country that illustrate the diversity and personality of *Real Life Decorating*. His passion and commitment to illustrating the best of innovative decorating made this book possible. He is a collector—of sleek, beautifully designed, mid-20th-century furniture, lamps, and accessories. His wall colors, green for a living room of 1940s bamboo furniture and turquoise blue for the dining room, reflect the period he collects. A special thank-you to the generous and gracious decorating enthusiasts who opened their homes and shared their ideas and sources with us. Rich and I both gleaned tremendous inspiration from the homes we visited— and we made new friends across the country. Have fun with *Real Life Decorating* and with your own projects. Please share your ideas and suggestions with us. My e-mail address is lhallam@mdp.com. *LH*

NAME: JEFFREY ALAN MARKS

LIFESTYLE: SINGLE; OWNS DESIGN FIRM

LOCATION: LA JOLLA, CALIFORNIA

DESIGN CHALLENGE:

A busy young designer tackles paring down his traditional style for the move from his first-home cottage to an open contemporary ranch.

carefree on the coast

Jeffrey updates with a light, white palette energized with jolts of bright color, such as the silk plaid. He designed the nickel fixture, with a mid-20th century shade, to match the house's contemporary spirit.

Jeffrey decorated by restricting color to
one key statement per room. In his guest
room, he focuses color on the striped
blue and green walls, which repeat his
second recurring theme of horizontal lines.

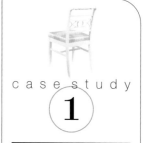

design is always on the move for Jeffrey Alan Marks. The energetic young designer filled his first home, a cottage of tiny rooms, with painted furniture, fabrics, and an array of flea market finds. His second home, a low-slung 1950s California ranch, inspires a new decorating direction that melds traditional furniture and art with mid-20th century design.

The sleeker, more contemporary mood evolved during the first months Jeffrey lived in the paneled house. "The house had never been changed; it had the original paint," Jeffrey says. "Before I moved in, I planned to do a French kind of thing, with the doors opening to the patio. But after I had lived in the house for a couple of months, I changed my mind."

During the interval, when he watched how light moved through the house, Jeffrey decided to take a lighter, more modern direction to the redesign and decorating. "The house called for clean lines of furniture, not a lot of decorating, not a lot of molding or fancy paint work," he says. "My tastes changed to fit the house."

For the background to this pared-down look, Jeffrey removed walls, added darkly stained hardwood floors, and cleaned up the rooms with white paint and new lighting. The dining area, *pages 13 and 24*, illustrates his current take on minimal traditional style with dark hardwood floors balancing the white walls, window treatments, and repainted chairs.

In the rooms where he interjects more color, such as the guest room, *opposite*, Jeffrey sets up a playful mood. He horizontally striped the walls in blue and green as lighthearted background for traditional pieces re-used from his cottage. The young designer also recycles furnishings, including a colorful striped padded screen for his own bedroom, *pages 20-21*. As a nod to color and comfort, the room pairs sunshine-yellow walls with blue, white, and yellow furnishings. The padded headboard and screen add touches of soft luxury to the personal space.

With the comfort of tradition in the bedrooms, Jeffrey explores modernist design in the open living room, *pages 16-19*. "I like the feel of the Delano Hotel in Miami Beach, a stark, clean, white look," he says. Inspired by the light-filled hotel, Jeffrey painted the ceiling with light-reflecting, high-gloss enamel.

> **"**
> traditional is still my style. but for this house, it's minimal traditional. if you have too much stuff, have a garage sale.
> **"**

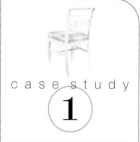

Walls are white with a pale, sea green accent wall, *opposite*. Furnishings mix pieces restyled from Jeffrey's first home with a dramatic, contemporary sectional sofa he designed for the living room. To update upholstered pieces, arranged in two conversation groupings, he removed skirts and re-covered them in more sophisticated fabrics. For a tailored milieu, collections are banished, old lamps updated with new shades, and rectangular mirrors hung as art. The horizontal lines of the stacked mirrors, *pages 18–19*, illustrate one of Jeffrey's design motifs for the house: emphasize the strongly horizontal to downplay the home's low ceilings.

Restricted color is another repeating theme. "I wanted each room to have a jolt of color," he says. Jeffrey enlivened the white dining room, *pages 13 and 24*, by upholstering the seats of the repainted chairs in a bright yellow plaid and hanging a modern landscape. He added orange to the scheme—painting the island base with automobile paint. "Orange takes the kitchen in a different direction," Jeffrey says. "It doesn't have anything to do with other colors in the house; it's unexpected. That's why I like it."

> **"**
> it's nice to put your collections away for a couple of years; then they feel new again. views are my art, not a lot on the walls.
> **"**

Jeffrey lightened up and pared down by painting the living room surfaces white and pale green. The damask armchairs and cylinder sconce shades epitomize the home's direction to minimal traditional.

" i designed the sectional sofa around the idea of the two corner windows. i wanted two separate sitting areas for parties. "

The sectional sofa returns. Jeffrey designed his own to mimic right angles of the corner windows. He also designed the framed rectangular mirrors to reinforce the strong horizontal lines of the ranch.

66

i keep the
room
backgrounds
simple.
everything in
my house
can be
moved
into another
room
and still
work for me.

99

Left: Jeffrey prefers a restful palette with soft colors when he designs bedrooms. In his own, pale yellow walls enliven blue and white furnishings from his cottage. Shutters control light without distracting pattern. *Top right:* A contemporary lamp and minimal accessories clean up the look. *Bottom right:* Horizontal stripes update a traditional harbor scene and spool-style poster bed in the guest room.

Jeffrey kept the original tile and some of the cabinets when he lightened the kitchen. The stainless steel island top contrasts with the bright orange base, painted with auto body paint.

orange takes the kitchen in a different direction; i wanted to add a jolt of color that had nothing to do with anything else.

Jeffrey cleans up pieces, such as the chairs, by painting with white boat enamel. His other residence, in Los Angeles, where he maintains a second design studio, is more traditional.

◆ **Clean up and repaint** country or cottage furniture for a more contemporary look. Sand to remove the remnants of peeling paint. Prime and repaint with shiny, white enamel. To enhance the shine, replace hardware with sleek, contemporary styles.

◆Incorporate traditional furnishings **in new, pared-down ways. Rethink and refine, not replace, are the keys to the minimal traditional look. Use fewer pieces, such as one rather than a pair of pedestal tables; minimize accessories; and hang one large painting.**

◆ **Respect your home's original** architecture and materials. Rather than tearing out kitchens and baths, plan decorating schemes that incorporate counters, tile work, cabinetry, or other items that are costly to replace. The results will save money and create rooms in harmony with the original style.

◆Ligthen walls and darken hardwood floors **for the most current look, an updated twist on classic black and white. The cleanest, freshest decorating balances open, minimized interiors with the stability of dark wood floors. The contrast creates a foil for furniture and art.**

◆ **Swap heavy metals,** such as ornate silver or traditional pewter, brass, or iron for the lighter, sleeker look of plain or brushed nickel. Choose well-shaped sconces, lamps, and accessories with minimal detailing—or display only one or two ornate objects from your collections.

NAME: CAMILO AND AURORA BARCENAS

LIFESTYLE: MARRIED; LARGE EXTENDED FAMILY

LOCATION: HOUSTON, TEXAS

DESIGN CHALLENGE:
This busy couple needs room for visiting children and family members and background colors that welcome art and artifacts collected on their travels.

love of latin heritage

White upholstery plays off rich cinnamon walls in the formal living room. One of the family's paintings by Nicaraguan artists hangs above the lacquered bench Aurora designed for her previous residence.

Calm colors, soft upholstery, and gently gathered draperies create a mood of serenity in the master sitting area off the bedroom. Black accents give a sophisticated touch.

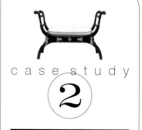

home is a haven of personal expression for Aurora and Camilo Barcenas, enriched by their love of the art, textiles, and tropical colors of their native Nicaragua. The traditional house that the couple built is also the gathering spot for their two professional daughters, son, and their extended families. "We have visiting family in and out," Camilo says. "My office staff calls our house 'Hotel Barcenas.'"

Neighbors in Managua, Aurora and Camilo grew up in an environment attuned to art. "People in Nicaragua collect art," Aurora says. "They may not buy furniture, but they buy art. I grew up surrounded by artwork created by my father who worked in different mediums."

The family's Houston home embodies such interests and experiences. "I think a house grows with you and reflects your personality," Aurora says. While her palette is a lively play of neutrals and saturated colors in the living room *pages 27, 30–31*, the hues of the master retreat are quiet and soothing. In the sitting room, *opposite*, off the bedroom, Aurora pairs a gray-blue wall color with blue-and-cream upholstery. She fills this private space with books, family photographs, and religious figures of the Virgin Mary. "They recall my childhood," she says. "I didn't know I had a collection until I counted."

Balancing the private calm of the master bedroom, the living room welcomes guests with warm cinnamon walls as the background for art, textiles, and sophisticated white upholstery. Here, the walls and art infuse the room with colors inspired by the Oriental rug, while the upholstery and draperies are purposefully neutral. This openness to strong color doesn't mean constant change. Instead, Aurora chooses backgrounds that work for changing art and collections through the years.

Favorite pieces in her personal style are the lacquered bench she designed years ago and a collection of miniature horses gathered on her travels with Camilo and their children. With her design eye, Aurora looks for horses in the same scale to canter gracefully across the mantel. Hanging above the horses is a major painting by Franco Penalba, one of the prominent Nicaraguan artists whose work the couple collects. While such art is her passion, Aurora points out that hanging a painting isn't easy.

66

the art of decorating is a tool to create harmony; harmony and comfort in a home are most important.

99

The Oriental rug introduces the living room's cinnamon wall color, a rich backdrop for paintings and collections. The carved pedestal table base anchors the room and balances the glass coffee table.

"Each piece has a strong personality. One painting doesn't necessarily play well with another." With each acquisition, she rearranges her artwork for gracious displays of paintings.

With their love of art, the family gravitates to a neutral palette for the family room, dining area, and kitchen, *pages 34–35.* "We knew we were going to add art," Aurora says. A favorite display technique contrasts a modern painting from her native country with stylized ceramic fruit by a Mexican artist.

The loggia, the family's fresh-air living room, *page 36,* also reflects diverse cultures. Aurora designed the table, bench, and chairs, crafted by Houston artisan David Solano. The bench and chairs are upholstered with woven tablecloths she bought in a market square in Peru.

In this fresh-air gathering spot, as throughout the house, Camilo and Aurora's goal is to create a place their children will always call home. "When we married and moved together to the United States 30 years ago, it was sad to leave home," Aurora says. "But my mother told me I would always have a home to visit. Now that's what we tell our children."

66

i'd rather buy art than a piece of furniture or a silver thing. buy art for yourself, to make you happy.

99

The sun-warmed wall color and cool white upholstery and draperies recall homes in tropical Central America. Collected textiles, including the gossamer table skirt, and pillows enliven with reds and golds.

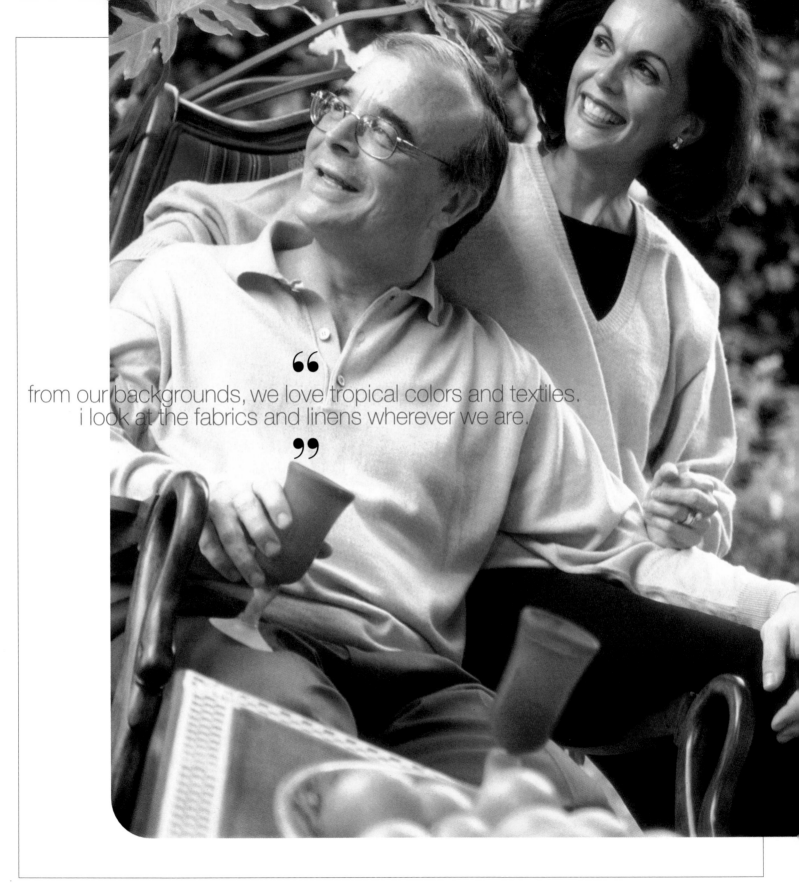

" from our backgrounds, we love tropical colors and textiles. i look at the fabrics and linens wherever we are. "

Right: Aurora chose white walls and cabinets so that art, such as the watercolors by a Nicaraguan artist, would be the focus of the family living area. *Top left:* A painting by Hugo Palma Ibarra pairs with oversized fruit and an antique wooden bowl from Guatemala. *Bottom left:* Aurora worked with skilled artisans in Mexico to create the look of an ornately carved, 19th-century wing-back armchair.

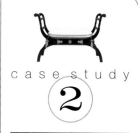

66

when i travel,
i go to the
galleries and
try to meet
the artists in
their studios.
i love to
see them
express
themselves
through their
creations.

99

In Houston's semi-tropical climate, the loggia serves as the fresh-air living and dining room. Textiles from Peru and a Mexican vase inspire the palette. Aurora's sister sculpted the stylized mask.

✦**Warm your rooms with versatile throws** and textiles. Temporary infusions of color and pattern allow you to change your rooms seasonally or for holidays, as Aurora does. Use warmer colors during the coolest months. Switch to serene greens and blues to cool down hot summers.

✦Get the maximum impact **from your chosen colors. Pair colorful walls with neutral upholstery and draperies in some rooms. Switch to neutral walls and colorful fabrics, art, and accessories in others. The contrast between walls, fabrics, and art creates visual energy.**

✦**Choose neutral colors without pattern** and tailored designs for window treatments that will work tastefully in your rooms through the years. For dressy looks for tiebacks, add delicate trims and tassels in subdued but regal textures and colors, such as copper, bronze, or aged golds.

✦Collect original art that's meaningful to you. **For a modest start, visit local art schools or artist cooperative galleries. (Some galleries rent so you can try out a piece.) Lean art against the wall to enjoy a piece before you make a commitment to hanging it.**

✦**Scale up when you collect** and shop for accessories. Fewer, larger pieces, such as these ceramic fruits, are more important and visually dramatic than vast collections of many small objects. Choose handcrafted containers, such as this carved antique dough bowl, for groupings.

DESIGN CHALLENGE:
These first-time homeowners face carving out space for a new baby, a home-based business, and friends in one small postwar house.

baby makes three

Judy and Malek energized the combination nursery/guest room with a ragged paint finish and bright pastel fabrics. They had a custom mattress made to turn an aged daybed into a reading and napping spot.

The pale turquoise ceiling reflects light and adds another attractive surface in the small dining room. Matching mats and frames unify collected etchings. Painted pottery below them enriches the grouping.

Malek and Judy Elkhoury plan an extensive addition to their small '40s house. Until they add on, the do-it-yourself couple uses clever decorating, recycling, and storage ideas to maximize their space and budget.

Color and fabrics are natural starting points for Judy, a professional seamstress who specializes in slipcovers, draperies, and other fabrications. In her own decorating, she gravitates to soft, velvety tones of warm, earthy wall colors and to the versatility of simple sewing projects. For the dining area, *opposite*, Judy translated her palette to a buff shade above the chair rail and to porcelain green below. The ceiling, painted a pale turquoise, reflects light. Judy relaxed the traditional dining table and chairs, good buys at a local antiques store, with a scalloped tablecloth she designed and made. The two-color fabric combination repeats the decorating idea of two wall colors—a quick and effective way to unify the room. For interesting art on a budget, Judy matted and framed etchings from a thrift store. The etchings hang neatly above an oblong basket and hand-painted pottery plates chosen for their texture and earthy hues.

Judy and Malek's formula of creativity plus hard work proves as effective in the living area, *pages 42–43, 46.* For a fresh background, they repeated the warm buff and turquoise used in the dining area and freshened the fireplace surround and woodwork with white paint.

Rather than buy new furniture, Judy had a club chair and ottoman re-covered and made slipcovers for a sofa and loveseat. In addition to stretching the budget, the slipcovers imbue the room with the friendly, easy-care ambience Judy and Malek want for guests and children. "We entertain a lot," she says. "The cotton duck for the sofa is great because I can pull it off and throw it in the washing machine." Pillows sewn from fabric remnants add color and pattern.

Storage and display contribute style as well as function. Judy and Malek substituted a pair of woven storage cubes for a conventional coffee table. Salvaged brackets support a painted gallery shelf to display artifacts and mementos.

The room comes to life with another of Judy's budget-stretchers—a quick window treatment inspired by brass letters from a flea market. "I wanted to finish the living room," she says.

> **"**
> use a lot of
> a quality but
> inexpensive
> fabric for
> draperies,
> buy just
> 1 yard
> of expensive
> fabric for
> pillows that
> have a lot of
> impact.
> **"**

Natural wood tones and white, punched up with colorful prints, freshen the living area. To make the print from a Santa Fe gallery larger, Judy made the deep mat from a crumbled brown paper bag.

"And I had a bolt of fabric I had bought for a dollar something at a yard sale." Shopping for a substitute to standard drapery rods, Judy stumbled on a bowl of old brass letters. She bought the letters, took them home, and played with combinations. "I figured out I had the letters to spell out 'Bon Ami,'" she says. That was perfect as "good friend," the English translation, symbolizes what they call their friendship corner.

Judy's imagination took a playful turn in the the hall and baby Elizabeth's nursery, *pages 44–45*, inspired by an English fabric of hand-drawn motifs and a coordinating plaid. "I fell in love with the colors in the print," Judy says. "The motifs reminded me of the circus. I took my design ideas from there." As a whimsical background, Judy talked Malek into helping her tape and paint horizontal stripes in the hall. In the nursery, she transformed plywood shelves into a wardrobe by crafting the tepee-style cornice from the print fabric and sides from plaid panels on brass rods. The plaid, made into a bumper pad, updates Judy's own baby crib. For a happy ending, she sewed a Roman shade and detailed it with glass-bead trim.

66

we decorated our living room for children. we slipcovered the sofa and loveseat in a cotton duck we could throw in the wash.

99

Judy insisted on painting wide horizontal stripes in the hall leading to the vibrant nursery. She based the colors on the fabrics.
Opposite: A fabricated, tepee-style cornice and panels turn shelving into a wardrobe for storage and display.

the stripes on the hall wall tested our relationship.
we had to plumb the
horizontal lines and mask off everything.

In her quest for pretty color, Judy painted the ceiling a pale turquoise. Brass letters, attached to the wall on hooks, suspend drapery panels. White duck modernizes the sofa; pillows are from fabric remnants.

✦ **Update old chairs** with slipcovers in simple, basic shapes. Tailored designs are easier to sew and easier to assemble if you are matching plaids, stripes, or prints. Sturdy, washable fabrics, with self-cording for trim, are more economical than slipcovers that have to be dry-cleaned.

✦ Buy one or two top-quality accessories **and mix them with collectibles from tag sales and flea markets. An obviously well-made lamp with a linen shade or classic candlesticks are pieces that will elevate the tone of any grouping.**

✦ **Create vignettes by planning** tabletop and wall displays as one arrangement. Craft a display shelf by hanging aged brackets for supports. Hang plates and small artwork to the sides and under a display shelf to fill the space. White plates add shapes and design without distracting color.

✦ Find new uses for old pieces. **Cut or buy a plywood round to top a battered cabinet or small table for a new shape. Conceal and skirt with a decorative print or vibrant solid fabric, or a round cloth plus overlay, for an instant designer look.**

✦ **Hang fabric panels** on wire lines suspended from the ceiling if you are desperate to add concealed storage in a room. Choose complementary washable cotton fabrics, such as the two gingham checks here, for a pleasing look that doesn't strain your decorating budget.

NAME: DEBORAH BISHOP AND MICHAEL LIEBERMAN

LIFESTYLE: MARRIED IN THE CITY

LOCATION: SAN FRANCISCO, CALIFORNIA

DESIGN CHALLENGE:
A dedicated collector and a pared-down contemporary aficionado dare to meld styles and possessions in their sophisticated city house.

opposites attract

Velvet draperies, dip-dyed by a Santa Fe
textile artist, pillows, and throws warm the
living room. The Moroccan-style lantern
and tables, with mosaic tops, contribute
exotic shapes to the personal design.

The generously sized stainless steel dining table pairs with reproduction mid-century-style chairs. Deborah scours flea markets for period collectibles, such as these colorful portraits by unknown artists.

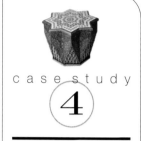

An urban pioneer in San Francisco's reviving South Park neighborhood, Michael Lieberman converted a boarded-up, abandoned hotel into his bachelor residence. The project was so involved and extensive that the San Francisco lawyer worked with structural engineer Rajenda Sahai and architect Alan Rudy to transform a derelict structure into an open, light-filled house. Michael minimized color and furniture with white walls and contemporary finds, such as Eames and Herman Miller chairs. Enter Deborah Bishop, who owned a classic painted San Francisco Victorian house, brimming with color, furnishings, and collections. "Even before I met Michael, I loved the neighborhood," she says. "It's an interesting mix of businesses and residences, very European." She enjoyed the location with its two terraces, a garden, and the beautifully crafted kitchen, but she found the pristine house bland and empty. "Love does conquer all. I couldn't live in it like it was, and I had all this stuff. That's where the fun began."

As did the starting point of the ying and yang and point-counterpoint of their different styles.

When Deborah moved in, she was on a book deadline and too busy to tackle anything but the office. So the couple started off with the industrial furniture from the 1940s and 1950s and layered on color. When time pressures eased, they bought a sofa for the living room and shoved tables together so they could entertain. Instead of immediately hanging artwork, Deborah and Michael introduced color and texture with Italian-style stucco. They warmed the open living room, *pages 49, 52–53*, with dip-dyed velvets created by a Santa Fe textile artist.

As they layered on colors and textures, the couple began to consult designer Marion Philpotts. "With our different tastes, it helped to have a third person as a mediator, a sounding board," Deborah says. In the dining area, *opposite*, their sensibilities create an intriguing space. The long stainless steel table, chosen for entertaining, and reproduction mid-century-style steel chairs create a sleek backdrop for Deborah's funky oil portraits found at area flea markets.

As they shared the house, Michael and Deborah slowly colored in the palette, moving from white and black to rich shades of orange,

> 66
> i found the
> street and
> stumbled on
> the building.
> it's been
> 10 years of
> work with
> long gaps in
> between.
> 99

> we don't like
> things that
> rigidly
> adhere to
> one style or
> another.
> things do
> work
> together,
> and themes
> do marry
> over time.

fennel green, blue, and red. "I felt the house needed color," Deborah says. "I'm a believer in mixing things up. I like things that clash, colors that clash." Michael savors the changes in his once-serene house. "I was always adverse to color," he says. "But now I enjoy what it does."

Enriching the house included working with craftsman Philip Agee to add bookcases and a mantel for the living room and tables for the bedroom, *pages 56–57*. "We have lots of books so the bookcases are a big issue for us," Deborah says. "Books are our most interesting things; we feel strongly about living with them."

She takes a more insouciant approach to decorative accents. For a sitting area, *opposite*, Deborah hung an exotic lantern and added Moroccan tables purchased in San Francisco. Her collections, pared down from her Victorian house, are also finding homes. "I starting buying paint-by-number paintings of Parisian landmarks; they are so classic in a kitschy way," she says. "Friends started giving them to me. I don't take them seriously." In a house with such strong design bones, the marriage of contemporary and collectible is indeed a happy one.

" we had two different aesthetics. i could become a bit cluttery; michael is a bit austere. we pushed to a better place. "

Opposite: Italian-style stucco enriches the walls with a mix of saturated colors and textures. Deborah warms the open plan with reds and yellows. *Left:* Glassware from local shops mixes with colorful vases and an array of candles on the steel table.

case study

④

―――――

" our house is
a work in
progress. we
aren't in a
big rush
to finish, but
we love
where it's
going with
more color.

"

Left: Dip-dyed velvet draperies give a sense of enclosure to the master bedroom, furnished with a leather bed, maple laboratory cabinet as chest, and custom Philip Agee bench. *Top right:* Michael added a terrace off the master bedroom when he renovated. The steel dining set epitomizes sleek European design. *Bottom right:* Deborah groups her collection of paint-by-number Parisian landmarks in the guest room.

Designed as a contemporary space of sleek materials, the open kitchen incorporates contemporary classics, such as the tractor-seat-style stool. Deborah hung the Chinese lanterns for accents.

✦**Incorporate mid-century modern** into your decorating. Michael's parents owned this classic Herman Miller rocker. If family pieces aren't in the picture, shop vintage furniture stores that specialize in such classics. Or try upscale consignment shops (See Sources pages 158–165 for ideas.)

✦Slow down and consider **working with a professional designer when you are melding decorating styles. Use the** designer's **professional eye to blend possessions and collections. Buy some new pieces together to forge your new home.**

✦**Include finishing touches from exotic** cultures for a sophisticated setting. And buy these special pieces when you see them. Deborah found her Moroccan-style lanterns years ago when a neighborhood shop was going out of business. Now they pair with dip-dyed velvet draperies.

✦Take a lighthearted approach **to collecting and decorating. Deborah enjoys searching thrift store and flea markets for affordable icons of popular culture, such as paint-by-number "art" and memorabilia with a sailor theme, easy to find in her port city of San Francisco.**

✦**Warm with textiles and saturated colors.** Use draperies to create defined areas in open plans and contemporary settings. Fabrics in rich colors take the stark edge off contemporary settings. Work with subdued patterns and touches of color to enliven without competing with architecture.

NAME: CAROLYN AND TOM CARROLL

LIFESTYLE: MARRIED; CHILDREN GROWN

LOCATION: LITTLE ROCK, ARKANSAS

DESIGN CHALLENGE:
These avid collectors search for the space and neutral wall colors to display the rich fruits of their years of antiquing and collecting.

filling the empty nest

Carolyn creates distinctive vignettes by freely mixing British and French pieces, such as the woven Orkney chair from Scotland with a French armchair and unglazed olive oil jar.

Whitewashed rough cedar siding gives a textured, clean backdrop for a pair of French chairs and a table Tom crafted from an old pine base. Antique cobbler forms, collected through the years, line the stairs.

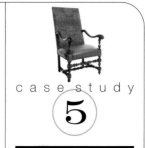
Carolyn Carroll describes herself as a born collector. But she and her husband, Tom, had to wait until they had educated their three children to actively pursue their interests. "I think collecting is in your blood. When you are a collector, it is something that you want to do," she says. Carolyn started with blue-and-white porcelains. From her first small plate, she was hooked and bought pieces she saw and could afford. Then a friend gave her a glazed mud man figure from China. With that one piece, she had a new interest. "Collecting is like that," she says. "You become aware of something; it appeals to you; then you start noticing it."

When the couple lived in Dallas, Carolyn had on-the-job training in design and antiques as an assistant for a design firm. During those years, she and Tom began collecting chairs, different types of accessories, old leather books, and boxes. And they developed an interest in European styles and accessories, particularly the sun-warmed textures and colors of Country French. When Tom was transferred to Little Rock, their collecting took a turn to the serious. With more time and disposable income, they

included small oil paintings. And Tom learned to convert and wire pottery, candlesticks, and assorted objects for one-of-a-kind table lamps.

With their ever-growing collections, the couple remodeled their suburban house for a more open plan—and appropriate backdrops. "You have to have the background and palette for your collections," Carolyn says. They ripped out the inexpensive wall paneling and, where they could, added rough cedar, whitewashed for texture. In the sitting room/library, *page 61*, originally the dining room, they warmed the ceiling with the rough cedar and added a wall of French doors and decorative wall sconces. The doors—and garden outside—frame a drop-leaf table of favorite European collectibles. This table, with distinctive barley twist legs, and the table Tom crafted from an old base, *opposite*, illustrate Carolyn's talents for grouping diverse objects by varying scale and elevations. Both settings also incorporate her collected chairs. "I like pairs when I can find them, such as the French chairs," she says. "But it's much easier to find a lone chair, which is usually a good buy." When she mixes chairs, Carolyn looks for a common

Passionate collectors need organized display. Carolyn designed built-ins around and over the cased opening between the living and sitting rooms. Shelf heights vary for larger objects.

"
i'm a chair freak. i can't stop collecting them. i use all
of mine for seating at christmas dinner.
"

The entry gives a
preview of the
interesting
collectibles to come.
One overscale piece,
here a reproduction
trumeau (pictorial)
mirror, anchors a
diverse grouping
and plates.

design element. In the sitting room, the scale of the chairs is similar although the materials and origins are different. In the entry, *left*, the rounded shapes allow a Louis XVI-style straight chair and a tufted Edwardian-style English chair to co-exist with a reproduction trumeau (pictorial frame) mirror.

Organization helps smaller objects to achieve such design harmony. In the living room, with pale terra-cotta walls, *pages 64–65*, Carolyn and Tom added built-in bookcases to display and organize their many collections. "When you are a collector, built-ins make a huge difference," Carolyn says. "There are only so many tabletops you can decorate in a house, and tabletop after tabletop gets to be too much."

Which is not to say a collector should hang on to everything, she adds. "Tom and I have been doing this for a long time. You upgrade as you go along. Through the years, we have replaced or traded or sold things. As you learn more about what you are collecting, your tastes refine. I collect because I love something. I'm not bothered by a chip or small crack. If I had to collect just the perfect, it wouldn't be fun anymore."

66

we don't collect for investment; we collect because we love it. chips don't bother me; signs of age make things more interesting.

99

"

while tom works on lamps, his friends keep him company in the workshop watching sports on television.

"

Left: For a Country French mood in the family room, roosters on aged brackets flank an oil painting of farm life. Slipcovers, in lively red-and-white stripes, unify upholstered pieces.

Top right: Repetition of like objects imparts immediate impact. New and old blue-and-white group with a painted mirror frame.

Bottom right: Changes in height make objects more important. Tom crafted the lamp from a candlestick.

A table lamp, converted from a trophy, lights the guest room/library. A pair of transferware plates and an oval metal tray contribute diverse shapes and textures to a neatly arranged grouping.

◆ **Look for interesting, one-of-a kind** objects that can be made into table lamps at a lamp shop. Use decorative mounting and attach to a base when it's impractical to drill holes for wiring. Dress up a shade with hand-sewn or hot-glued trim. (Beaded trim is a fashionable look.)

◆ Collect objects, **such as painted metal tole trays, plates, old leather books, boxes, baskets, and unframed paintings, for backdrops and elevations. Include salvaged wall brackets and fragments in your antiquing for an extra display dimension.**

◆ **Pick a theme with easy-to-find motifs** and objects for a quick starting point. For quick Country French, look for the farm animals (roosters and pigs are appropriate) often associated with the style. Display prized finds, such as this glazed pottery rooster, on brackets for emphasis.

◆ Keep your eyes open to chair possibilities. **Odd chairs that strayed from a set are good buys. Shop for shape and construction, not finish or fabric, which can be changed. A well-made secondhand chair is a better long-term investment than a cheap new one.**

◆ **Group cultures and continents** for harmony. Delicate Oriental accessories, such as the Japanese Imari plate and elevated Chinese mud men figures, mix easily with the rich colors of leather-bound books—and the refinement of blue-and-white Chinese export porcelains.

NAME: GWEN, JACK, COLIN, AND BRITA HAUSER

LIFESTYLE: CHILDREN—COLLEGE AND HIGH SCHOOL

LOCATION: SAINT PAUL, MINNESOTA

DESIGN CHALLENGE:
Mom, dad, and
the two kids want to redo
their older house for
color, comfort, and style,
but investing in
education comes first.

the family project

Gwen's desire for sun prompted the warm color choice for the dining area. She repainted a 1920s table and shield-back chairs and stenciled Swedish culinary terms for a Country Scandinavian look.

Colors for the painted tabletop repeat the plaid that re-covers a spoon-carved bench, crafted from an antique bed. The family moved the cabinet from the original dining room.

*g*wen Hauser is stubborn. She wanted a pretty, comfortable house for her family, and she refused to be stifled by a modest budget. "My creative energy came from a lack of funds," she says. When the family couldn't afford to wallpaper the living room, she figured out how to get the look she wanted with paint. From that modest beginning, Gwen, then a stay-at-home mom, began doing decorative painting for clients. When she needed to experiment with techniques, she worked at home, and as her work evolved, she slowly decorated her family's 80-year-old Dutch Colonial house.

After years of work, Gwen's art and style are beautifully displayed in the kitchen and dining area, *opposite*, the home's most dramatic plain-to-painted transformation. As a starting point, she created her own informal, country version of a Scandinavian kitchen. For ideas to inspire her, Gwen made collages using magazine clippings of what she liked. Sunny, yellow walls were the only givens. "I decided to paint in February in defiance of the long, gray winter," she explains. "We couldn't afford to escape to a warmer climate, so I painted all the sunshine I needed."

For motifs to paint, Gwen found a cheerful fabric with yellow tones, then mixed in three other patterns. From the fabrics, Gwen created the designs for the painted table and dining chairs, all bargain finds she had previously purchased and painted for another decorating scheme. The table and chairs are a sturdy 1920s reproduction set, originally stained. The chairs feature the shield-back design reminiscent of Scandinavian interpretations. Gwen looked through a Scandinavian cookbook, a reminder of her Swedish grandmother, to find the words.

With so much visual activity in the dining area, she strengthened the design by painting a "rug" in the same colors on the kitchen floor. And she found a small, vintage, marble-top Eastlake-style table to work as the island.

The original living and dining rooms, in their formal plan, didn't work for the family. So Gwen and Jack gave them different uses. They turned the dining room into her office, with an armoire for the family's shared computer. Gwen painted and glazed the walls and decoratively painted the baseboards. At the same time, they transformed the living room into a library/game

> **"**
>
> beyond choosing a style or a period, the colors, curves, and angles you enjoy are clues to what you like.
>
> **"**

> 66
>
> i wanted wallpaper in the living room. we couldn't afford it. so in my stubbornness, i made my own with paint.
>
> 99

room. Gwen's father built the simple bookcases, which she painted. Instead of a sofa, she bought four club chairs to group with a round table she crafted and painted from a family heirloom butcher block, *right*. Brita's artwork from school hangs above the bookcase.

After more than 20 years of living in the house, Gwen finally took on the master bedroom. Her inspiration: a rug with colors and shapes in the spirit of famous French artist, Henri Matisse. Gwen worked with her father to make the headboard from a fragment and the mantel that conceals the radiator. She painted the walls purple, a color she had never used, and finished them with a crackle technique.

Gwen sewed a duvet cover from sheets, then stenciled a design she copied from the rug. Fabric markers give the effect of hand-blocked linen. Brita's room is another study in vibrant color—deep blue. Gwen and Brita, who take art classes together, worked out the design during a family vacation. Back at home, they painted stripes on the walls and ceiling. "Our family creativity lives on," Gwen says. "When I look at our home, I see all the years and memories."

Originally the living room, the library features glazed green walls as a backdrop to Brita's unframed art school canvases. Gwen painted the tabletop, cut to fit an inherited butcher block.

"
part of the fun is the father-daughter relationship. i design what
i want, and dad builds it. it's not perfect, but it's charming.
"

Gwen's father crafted the bedroom mantel and headboard; she decorated the duvet with fabric markers. *Opposite:* A storage cabinet conceals the computer in the office. Gwen glazed the walls and added halogen fixtures.

❝

brita chose
the fabric
for the duvet
cover and
sham. then
we sketched
out ideas
for the walls.

❞

Left: Brita's small bedroom comes alive with ragged stripes and touches of yellow. The decorative trellis hides the radiator. *Top right:* Gwen practiced for a large commission by hand lettering the stair landing with literary quotes. *Bottom right:* The shared upstairs family bath takes on new life with painted beaded board and open storage. Gwen stenciled the cheerful fish and seashells in lieu of wallpaper.

Gwen painted a bordered kitchen "rug" to visually balance the decorative dining area. A marble top Eastlake-style table substitutes for a kitchen island in the tight space.

✦**Conceal the utilitarian with style.** Rather than living with the exposed radiators that heat the family's older home, Gwen worked with her father to craft clever cover-ups, such as the decorative mantel in her master bedroom. She crackled the surface for the appropriate touch of age.

✦Switch and adapt rooms **instead of adding more space. When the family needed change, Gwen and Jack transformed their formal rooms into informal spaces with fresh paint, clever storage, and new and recycled furniture.**

✦**Incorporate your family heritage** into your decorating and find expert help when needed. When Gwen decided to paint Scandinavian food terms on her dining table, she flipped through the pages of an authentic cookbook to get the correct spellings for her choices.

✦Broaden your definition of antiques **for good buys in furniture. Gwen found the 19th-century-style, shield-back style chairs she likes in an affordable 1920s reproduction. Early 20th-century furniture is often less expensive and sturdier than reproductions made today.**

✦**Employ paint as a stylish** budget-stretcher. To save money through the years, Gwen paints the looks she wants. Instead of spending money on a stair runner and its installation, she taped off and stenciled the borders of a decorative runner. Topcoats of a water-based sealant ensure long wear.

NAME: KAREN G. CAMPBELL

LIFESTYLE: SINGLE; CONSULTING FIRM CEO

LOCATION: WASHINGTON, D.C.

DESIGN CHALLENGE:
A fan of architecture takes on dual challenges of restoring a 1929 Renaissance Revival house and creating a vibrant, updated palette.

glamour in the city

Karen used the chairs as the starting point for her living room design. Gold tones with accents of purple repeat as regal accents for the 1920s house. Karen collects art of and by African-American women.

Designs and materials influenced by
Africa, Morocco, and Tuscany meld in
Karen's inviting sitting room and kitchen.
The interiors of homes in Dar es Salaam,
Tanzania, inspired the stucco walls.

successful businesswoman and community leader who heads her own bi-coastal consulting firm, Karen Campbell approaches decorating with the organizational skills she brings to her life and work. She also captures the spirit of adventure that led her to volunteer and later manage economic development projects in East Africa, Egypt, and the Caribbean.

Karen's sense of adventure and love of architecture spurred the busy single professional woman to tackle renovating and decorating a large 1920s Renaissance Revival house—in an orderly, methodical fashion. "For years, I had been reading and clipping decorating magazines," she explains. "When I bought this house, I pulled out tear sheets of everything I liked and saved." Karen bought a notebook and created tabbed sections for each room to organize the tear sheets, then made a storyboard for the interiors by pinning up swatches of fabrics, pieces of surface materials, and pictures. The result is her road map for the entire decorating scheme.

With this thoughtful approach, she began the renovation where it would have the most impact—in the kitchen/sitting room, *opposite.*

Working with designer Jennifer Gilmer, Karen redid the kitchen—tearing out the old and building back with the surfaces, finishes, and appliances she wanted. "It was important for me to have an intimate place to dine and a comfortable place to sit within the kitchen," she says. "Decorating the kitchen was just as important as decorating the other rooms of the house."

Karen also turned her attention to the formal living and dining rooms, foyer, and entry hall—grand spaces in the house that had been masterfully detailed by well-known architect Henry Wardman. The starting point for the living room, *pages 88–89,* was a pair of chairs. "When I was living in my first house, I started buying things that appealed to me for my next house," she says. "These chairs didn't go with anything I had then, but I liked the lines. I actually built the living room around the chairs." Working from the shapely chairs, Karen found a sofa with sculptural lines and print upholstery to mix with the chairs. The sofa repeats the golden tones of the chairs in a different pattern and scale. To anchor the room, she shopped for an imported rug and tried several before she found

i love dishes and glassware and wanted to enjoy them. it's a shame to put beautiful things behind doors.

Karen balances the ornate architecture of the living room with large-scale furnishings and touches of bold pattern and color. The carved heads on the mantel are indicative of the 1920s Revival style.

the perfect fit. "The rug I chose surprised me," she says. "I laid this one out, and the whole room suddenly seemed bolder. Houses have their own personality. For decorating to work, you do what the house wants to do. This house needed stronger, bolder color than I imagined."

Karen also found the grand old house is accepting of art and artifacts from her collecting and travels. After visiting friends who collect art for an older house they restored in her neighborhood, Karen found another passion for her energies. She searches for original paintings that appeal to her and gravitates to depictions of women by African-American and Haitian artists to mix with art and artifacts from her travels.

Karen's interest in different cultures gives her home an eclectic feel—on an international scale. In her home office, *page 94*, the mix includes an Egyptian rug, masks from Mexico and Africa, an ottoman covered in an ancient Turkish kilim, a Southeast Asian water vessel, and a starkly beautiful black-and-white photograph of a woman from the Samburu tribe in Kenya. "It all works," Karen says. "Cultures speak to one another in my home."

> "
> if you like
> a piece of art
> or furniture,
> it will work.
> every piece
> in your
> house
> should have
> meaning
> for you.
> "

case study

7

> 66
>
> when you add color, a house is more playful; when you add an ottoman, it's comfortable to put your feet up.
>
> 99

Left: The contrast of green and white creates interesting visual energy in the formal dining room. Karen collects glassware in rich jewel tones. *Top right:* Cultures mix with dramatic results in the entry with an antelope head sculpture from West Africa contrasting with a Southeast Asian carving. *Bottom right:* Artist Anita Philyaw painted the canvas, left unframed to relax the grand dining room.

Karen merged her penchant for European-crafted kitchens of furniture-quality cabinets with the natural materials, including concrete, used in Tanzanian homes. *Opposite:* The beautifully rendered painting by LaShun Beal warms the sitting room.

"the amber glass tiles have an incredible iridescence. they play to my love of morocco."

Masks from Mexico group with a favorite African photograph by artist Phil Borges above a Sumatra daybed from Indonesia. An Asian water vessel on a stand and a Morrocan lantern add scale.

✦ **Work with what you love.** Motifs and materials inspired the textural quality of the kitchen surface materials, including the mosaic tile border above the counter. Keep backdrops neutral and earthy so design focus—here the stylized, mosaic leaf pattern—makes a strong visual impact.

✦Organize your decorating inspirations. **Clip every magazine page that appeals to you and organize them room by room into your own decorating notebook. Make your own storyboard with fabric swatches and material samples.**

✦ **Play up the interesting** and unusual. When one element is the star, minimize competing elements. Starting with the intricately carved mantel, a feature in the grand Renaissance Revival homes of the 1920s, Karen kept accessories—the playful inclusion of gargoyle bookends—to a minimum.

✦Hone in on a starting point **for each room. Build your room around an element that appeals to you—a piece of furniture, rug, fabric, or art. Choose major elements that play off your inspiration. Enrich with colorful accents, such as pillows and art.**

✦ **Translate ideas from books** and magazines. Karen's coffee-table books on Moroccan and Tuscan homes inspired the arched, full-length louverered shutters and decorative hardware of her pantry doors. The books also helped her decide on natural colors for the kitchen.

NAME: SHELBY AND EVAN SCHNEIDER

LIFESTYLE: MARRIED; FIRST HOUSE

LOCATION: SARATOGA SPRINGS, NEW YORK

DESIGN CHALLENGE:
This twenty-something couple found a house that fit their first-time buyer budget. Could they learn the skills to make its dark rooms seem like home?

newlywed bliss

Color enriches for the cost of a can of paint. A garage sale metal bed pairs with flea market finds. Vintage costume jewelry necklaces serve as tiebacks for simple drapery panels.

Decorative trim dresses up plain ready-made drapery panels. Slipcovers, made from outlet bargains, add style to a plain sofa and ottoman. The rug, from a home center, contributes pattern.

A fourth-floor walk-up apartment convinced Evan and Shelby Schneider to look for a house—and yard—of their own. "We didn't think we were going to be able to find a house we could afford," Shelby says. "It was a fluke we found this one."

The affordable house, built in the 1960s, offered space and the challenge of lightening rooms closed in by dark walls, busy wallpaper, and stained woodwork. As novices to home improvements, Evan and Shelby asked their friend, Donna Wendt, a design consultant and stylist, for ideas. Donna suggested a pale, youthful color scheme to open the living areas. And Shelby, who wanted one colorful room, decided on rich red walls, balanced by white draperies and linens, for the guest room, *page 97*.

Light colors are the tool that freshens the house, giving a unifying theme to the design. The living room, *opposite*, pale yellow with an undertone of beige, opens to a light green dining area, kitchen, and den. Evan and Shelby painted trim throughout in a crisp shade of linen white. "We didn't have any skills at first, but we learned as we went along," Evan says.

As they worked on the clean and fresh background, Shelby and Donna shopped fabric outlets for bargains in slipcover and drapery materials—and discount stores for ready-made draperies. The only major piece purchased for the house was the well-made, well-priced sofa, slipcovered in a youthful print.

The other key piece for the living room is an armchair Shelby purchased for her studio apartment before she and Evan married. "The chair was the first piece of furniture I bought on my own," she says. "When it went on sale, I bought it for the shape. I figured it was a timeless piece I could use for the next 30 years." Where they filled in with family pieces, the couple updated. The bench Evan's grandfather crafted to lift weights serves as a side table. To modernize a pass-along side chair, Shelby re-covered the seat with a leopard print fabric as a no-sew project. These projects pale in comparison to the room's piece de resistance—the transformation of the massive, dark, multishelf built-in from eyesore to focal point, *pages 100–101*. Evan and Shelby planned to ask the sellers to remove it as a condition for sale. Donna saw another option—

Shelby and Evan turned a dark-wood built-in into a focal point by removing some of the shelves and updating with white paint. The spare arrangement of clocks and wedding gifts adds a contemporary feel.

stylish display for Shelby's art, clocks, collections, and the couple's special wedding presents. She helped the couple remove most of the glass shelves, then prime and paint the piece to match the workwood. Shelby updated hinges with paint and replaced the drawer pulls.

They repeated the process to freshen the kitchen cabinets—taking off doors, sanding, priming, painting, and replacing hinges and hardware. (To finish the redo, they had new laminate countertops installed.)

The major dining area project, *page 103*, the window treatment, also called for professional help. To take advantage of the existing cornice and a pair of windows, Shelby hired a local seamstress to make a single large Roman shade for the double windows. As a finishing touch, Donna found a vintage chandelier for $85 on the e-bay auction site. New shades, $3 each at a local home center, update the piece.

The intense work quickly paid off. "It didn't feel like our home when we started; everything was dark and heavy," Evan says. "But it feels like home now. And we've learned a lot about sanding, painting, and hardware, too."

> "
> paint is cheap. we sanded, primed, and painted everything. evan wasn't a handyman before we started.
> "

Shelby and Evan invested in laminate countertops. They sanded, primed, and painted dark, stained cabinets and replaced hardware with brushed-nickel knobs. *Opposite:* Shades from a home center dress up a bargain flea market iron chandelier.

" the dining windows are visible from the living room so we invested in a window treatment that's the focal point of the house. "

In the family room, shutters, salvage at $3 each, hang above the wainscotting to display postcards and photographs. A slipcover revives a chair from apartment days; a wicker chest provides storage.

case study

8

◆ **Use your wedding presents every day.** Don't put away your good vases or save serving pieces for special occasions. Instead fill them with flowers from the market or your garden for a polished finishing touch. Remember the design rule of an odd number of elements for harmony.

◆Substitute accent pillows **from a linen outlet or discount store for pillow inserts—even if you plan to cover them with new fabric. You'll have two pillows for the price of one. As a further budget-stretcher, sew covers from remnants or oversize dinner napkins.**

◆ **Work in pale sepia and cream tones** for current, sophisticated wall groupings. Mix family photographs with vintage photography from thrift or antique stores. Grouped prints and photographs are visually pleasing when colors and materials of frames and mats blend or match.

◆For the most look for your money, **don't skimp on fabric yardage or quality workmanship. It's more effective to purchase** generous amounts of less-expensive, outlet fabrics and then pay for a professional seamtress to sew draperies and slipcovers.

◆ **Collect, collect, collect** for the affordable accessories that enhance the personal style of your home. The secret: scour flea markets and tag and garage sales for items, such as these alarm clocks, that appeal to you. Narrow your collecting to a material or color and group for instant impact.

NAME: EMILY MINTON

LIFESTYLE: SINGLE; FREELANCE PHOTOGRAPHER

LOCATION: ATLANTA, GEORGIA

DESIGN CHALLENGE:
A globe-trotting photographer braves transforming a bland townhouse into a backdrop for her diverse furnishings and art.

mixing with the exotic

A mirror leaned against the wall reflects the view in Emily's living room. On the mantel, the delicate Masai figure from Kenya balances the carved Mexican dance mask. Emily collects Turkish kilim rugs.

French pieces—the leather-clad banquette and farm table—anchor the dining area. Emily stretched an Indian cotton textile to visually balance the kilim rug. A simple pendant illuminates the scene.

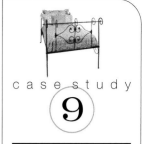

Emily Minton saw potential, not perfection, in the mid-1980s townhouse she bought for her home and office. While the townhouse didn't offer interesting architecture and vintage charm, its location, price, and natural light convinced the young freelance photographer to take a look. Emily knew with work and time she could create a compatible backdrop for her collected furniture and diverse collections.

After years of traveling around the world, her interests and tastes encompass a variety of styles and cultures. "I wanted my home to respect all different types of design—Indonesian, African, Turkish, French," Emily explains. "My goal was to find a way to pull it all together in harmony so every piece was elevated with interesting contradictions and no brazen mistakes." As starting points, Emily had the givens of several French pieces, including the French farm table, *opposite*, and kilim rugs from Turkey. The large French pieces anchor the furniture plan while the kilim rugs, purchased on two trips to Turkey, establish the earthy palette.

To make the living and dining areas and kitchen feel as open as possible in a small town-house, she chose the same shade of warm tan paint. Decorative painter Brian Carter ragged the walls for subtle texture. In the living room, *pages 107, 112–113*, Emily intensified colors with custom-made chartreuse silk draperies. "The chartreuse is a little trendy, but I pulled the color from a kilim rug in that room," Emily says. "I like the way that silk dresses up the room a little without going overboard."

The dressy touch is appropriate for a room filled with meaningful furniture and art from Turkey, Peru, Mexico, Kenya, and Indonesia. To the right of the French armoire is the religious art she collects—pieces from Peru, Mexico, and Ireland. On the mantel, Emily displays a carved African Masai figure. A quill box, willed to her from a family friend, is arranged with Turkish pots on a coffee table from her father's furniture line, the Minton-Corley collection.

In her bedroom, *pages 114–115*, Emily pulled a rich golden mustard color from a kilim rug for the walls. "I wanted the room to be brighter, more vibrant than the living area, a bit like Morocco," she says. The color enlivens the wood tones in the bedroom—from the Balinese

A printed spread from a Kenyan market dresses a bed found at an estate sale; the cornice is Italian. The matted photographs are from Emily's recent trip to Africa.

wood carving attached to the wall as a head-board to a 19th-century Texas-made writing table and American Empire chest.

Color takes a cooler twist in the combination guest room/study/office, *opposite.* For a starting point, Emily used the hand-blocked English linen pillows, pulling out a shade of dusty gray blue for the walls. The coverlet is an Indian bed-spread she found in a Kenyan street market. "I already had the pillows and the idea," she says. A Gothic Revival-style chair contributes one of the quirky touches Emily likes to add.

She also introduced the no-sew fabric hanging for the iron daybed, found at an auction. The hanging is from a muslin fabric she used every-where in her last house. Here, she draped it, clamped it to the cornice, and cut and puddled it. Because she doesn't sew, Emily cut window treatment panels from natural burlap, fraying the ends and applying fabric glue. The payoff: a home with her personal style and sensibilities. "For most of the things I've bought, I remember the faces of the people I've bought them from," Emily says. "It's really for me about respect for people and their cultures."

> **"**
> you need a
> starting point
> for every
> room. i drew
> the dusty
> blue for my
> office from
> the hand-
> blocked
> pillows.
> **"**

Right: Strong design marks Emily's style. The iron console is from her father's furniture collection; she added the limestone top. Cording, threaded through grommets, holds throw-style slipcovers in place. *Top left:* Carved lamp bases from Mexico pair with stitched leather shades that recall Emily's Texas heritage. *Bottom left:* Collected religious art groups with a French amoire.

"

no one
makes
furniture like
the french.
the
backbone of
my look
starts with
french and
goes quirky
from there.

"

A 19th-century Texas-made table and American Empire chest anchor a room of collectibles—a tobacco drying basket from the South, bamboo ladder, basket, and Indian textile folded as a coverlet.

> 66
>
> my decorating has a sentimental side. the table
> is covered in fabric that
> belonged to my great-grandmother in texas.
>
> 99

A lampshade from the mid-20th century contrasts with the cloisonné base, set on a table skirted with printed floral fabric inherited from Emily's great-grandmother. Kenyan candlesticks hold beeswax candles.

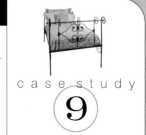

✦**Collect your passion.** Emily and her father search secondhand and antiques stores and flea markets for cameras of all styles and eras. For the most impact, she groups them on a table against a wall-hung architectural fragment, elevating a favorite vintage view camera for interest.

✦Make your bed. **Emily elevated a bed frame on cinder blocks for a pleasing height. For a one-of-kind headboard, she hung a Balinese wood carving on the wall. You don't have to journey to Bali for the look; a wood screen from an import store works, too.**

✦**Look for fabrics** that give choices for your wall colors—and be open to choices. Even though Emily does not use blue frequently, she loved the English hand-blocked linen she made into pillow covers. A pretty dusty blue shade in one of the pillows proved to be the color to paint her office wall.

✦Add texture to your decorating scheme. **Think beyond carpet. Emily replaced upstairs raspberry shag carpet with wall-to-wall sisal for a budget-stretching alternative to installing wood. And she ragged the living room walls for depth without distracting pattern.**

✦**Pack and ship your finds,** such as this vase. After backpacking for weeks with a kilim rug, Emily understood the advantage of shipping home. To ensure her bargains arrive safely, she either packs or watches the packing and then ships them herself. She limits herself to unusual, one-of-kind items.

NAME: DOROTHY, WILLIAM, AND BILLY BOGER

LIFESTYLE: MARRIED; TODDLER, BABY ON THE WAY

LOCATION: SUBURBAN, VIRGINIA

DESIGN CHALLENGE:
Before baby makes four, a young family settles in the suburbs. Their quest: updating a '60s ranch for the casual charm of their former urban townhouse.

moving to the burbs

Colorful kitchen tiles set the dining room's earthy color mood. Reproduction pieces—the cabinet and black chairs—update an inherited oak table. The sunburst motif reinforces the home's resort-style theme.

Converted from formal living space, the library features a new window seat that substitutes for a sofa. Built-in walnut bookcases organize inherited books and family memorabilia to minimize clutter.

As busy young professionals, Dorothy and Bill Boger restored a narrow three-story townhouse while their close-in neighborhood went from affordable to fashionable. Two terriers and a baby later, the townhouse was crowded but convenient to their city jobs. With the second baby on the way, they needed more space and off-street parking. Eventually they found a multilevel suburban house with a two-car garage. And they met designer Patrick Sutton, who helped them focus remodeling and decorating on how they live and entertain.

Though the house they bought was nicely decorated, it was more formal than Dorothy and Bill wanted. After years of vacationing in Florida, they envisioned an open home with a resort feel. And they wanted a house where dogs and children could play without worrying about carpets, furniture, and accessories.

As a starting point to a whole-house redo, Dorothy turned to the kitchen, *page 128*, the room that needed the most work. "I like to cook, and we entertain at home, so the kitchen is important to us. Patrick worked with us on the space planning to make it convenient." As the kitchen is much more than a utilitarian space, the designer suggested genuine linoleum, with a decorative inset, for the floor. Dorothy and Bill chose the Sun Valley, Idaho, sun motif for an inset with the yellow inspiring the wall color. Dorothy worked with a Key West tile shop, a source found on vacation, for the backsplash.

The warm earthy colors from the kitchen set the palette for the adjoining terra-cotta dining room, library (originally the living room), and entry. To relax the dining room, *page 119*, the couple replaced a chandelier with a glass-and-iron fixture and hung simple ready-made cotton draperies from black iron rods. Reproduction painted chairs from a home furnishings catalog pair with an inherited oak pedestal table.

Rather than allocating space to a living room they would rarely use, Dorothy and Bill worked with a cabinetmaker to design a window seat and built-in walnut bookcases, *opposite*, for Bill's inherited books. To comfortably furnish the room in library spirit, they shopped for a pair of 1940s-style leather chairs and an ottoman from a home furnishings store and added a console table, drink table, and retro-

> **"**
> we had to nail our bookcases to the wall in the townhouse. built-ins are a lot safer when you have young children.
> **"**

10

i'm not a
collector, but
i can't
pass up
wire models
of the
eiffel tower
after our
trip to france.

The library reflects the home's resort
theme. Black-and-white prints and
a banded sisal rug enhance the graphic
quality of the '40s-style leather chairs.
Collections are limited to Eiffel Towers.

style lamps from the same source. "We wanted to re-create the feel of a turn-of-the-century men's club," Bill says. "The warmth of the chairs and bookcases sets a relaxing mood for reading or conversation."

For art, the Bogers went with graphic style and history rather than provenance and chose prints of Library of Congress photographs, *right*. The archival prints are 16×20 inches, matted and framed to 24×28 inches.

The same relaxed mood travels upstairs to four-year-old Billy's vibrant blue room and the sea green master bedroom, *pages 126–127*. The bedroom, designed around a reproduction iron bed and armoire for the television, exudes the cool charm of the tropics. Windows are dressed simply in ready-made panels on black iron rods. Yellow linens present sunny contrast to the sea-inspired blue-green walls. For a final resort touch for the bath, Dorothy found a shower curtain sewn from a vintage, 1940s-style Florida souvenir map tablecloth. The result is an easy living house for now. "We don't want rooms that are off limits," Dorothy says. "Our priority is to enjoy our house and family."

REAL LIFE 122

Terra-cotta walls relax the dining room and complement the sunburst from a friend's vacation in Italy. The wall below the window is painted white for the allusion of French doors to the garden.

" this is a house for us right now, for children and terriers. we're saving the fancy stuff for later. "

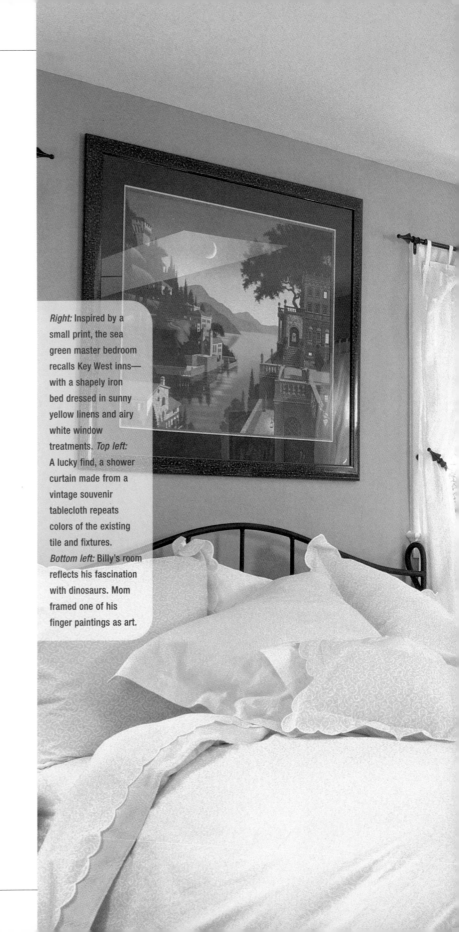

Right: Inspired by a small print, the sea green master bedroom recalls Key West inns— with a shapely iron bed dressed in sunny yellow linens and airy white window treatments. *Top left:* A lucky find, a shower curtain made from a vintage souvenir tablecloth repeats colors of the existing tile and fixtures. *Bottom left:* Billy's room reflects his fascination with dinosaurs. Mom framed one of his finger paintings as art.

"

the easy,
laid-back
style and the
colors of the
florida
keys appeal
to us.
that's how
i wanted
our bedroom
to feel.

"

Tiles from Key West, in a palm tree theme, and the Sun Valley sun as a linoleum inset remind Dorothy and Bill of vacation spots. The table and mismatched chairs are family pass-alongs from Louisiana.

◆ **Pick a theme and a color scheme** when you are remodeling or decorating. Dorothy and Bill saw the tiles in a Key West tile shop that jump-started the kitchen remodeling and their earthy color scheme. Small touches, such as this backsplash inset, can be enough to create your look.

◆Update inherited and family pass-along **furniture with well-made furnishings from national catalog retailers. Look for stylish, contemporary rugs and lamps with clean modern lines. Pair old dining tables with new painted chairs for a fresh look.**

◆ **Visit the websites** or make personal visits to the United States Library of Congress, the John F. Kennedy Library in Boston, and other libraries or historical societies with photography collections. See page 165 for further information on ordering from the Library of Congress and Kennedy Library.

◆Let in the light and minimize **window treatments. Replace heavy draperies with blinds or shades for privacy and sun control. When coverage isn't an issue, hang simple unlined cotton or linen drapery panels or sheers from black iron rods.**

◆ **Investigate flooring options,** such as authentic linoleum—back on the market for home remodeling. This sturdy material is easy to maintain and stands up to rigors of family life. Check with floor installers or kitchen designers for companies that do insets, such as this Sun Valley design.

Real life decorating is knowing the rules—and being brave enough to break them. Real life decorating is working with the colors that appeal to you—in the intensities that work with your setting, room style, and possessions. And it's learning how to mix—and sometimes match— furniture, art, and accessories to design a look tailored to your home and lifestyle. Use this illustrated style primer as a starting point to the basics of decorating. Turn to the sources and credits for shops, upscale consignment stores, and outlets that provide innovative ideas and stylish products.

style primer

COLOR & PAINT

PROPORTION & SCALE

FURNITURE & FLOOR PLANS

ART & ARRANGING

PATTERN & FABRIC

ACCESSORIES & COLLECTIONS

LIGHTING & LAMPS

STORAGE & DISPLAY

SOURCES & RESOURCES

COLOR & PAINT

Change the palette and feel of any room with a gallon or two of paint—or a few well-chosen accessories. How do you get the most from this amazing tool? Recognize your color preferences and resolve to live with what you love. Look through your clothes closet for your favorite colors. Or scan the pages of this book. Think on the practical side, too. If you already own a sofa or rug you need to use, pull out a color and repeat it for the background. To use colors as designers do, work with those of the same value (intensity). If you prefer a scheme based on a single color, choose one you enjoy and vary the tones from paler tints to dark shades throughout your home. Employ the dark tones for areas that anchor and create focus, such as wainscoting under chair rails, or the fireplace wall.

WARM COOL HUES WITH RED

Spin the color wheel for your color palette. Lavender and green on the cool side of the spectrum soothe a cottage-style bedroom. Touches of red, adjacent to purple on the color wheel, give a lively counterpoint and jolt of energy.

style
(1)
primer

Pair the warm hues of yellow and red for a happy color scheme. Decorators gravitate to sunny yellow for walls, especially in bedrooms, to take advantage of the color's light-reflecting qualities. Red supports for playful accents.

ENERGETIC RED AND YELLOW

COLORS OF CONTEMPORARY

Give contemporary a playful twist with bright pastels, such as turquoise and hot pink, popularized in the 1980s by television's "Miami Vice." With the current interest in mid-20th century modern design, the combo is hot again.

COLOR & PAINT

Blue and white rank as the most beloved of two-color palettes. A mix of patterns that varies the hues of the blues enlivens this classic scheme. Quilts and accessories, in white and blue, finish in refreshed style.

style ⑤ primer

CLASSIC BLUE AND WHITE

FRESH AND LIVELY

style ④ primer

Update classic yellow and green with lively tints of these favorite colors. A youthful slant pairs pale yellows with light apple green, which has undertones of yellow. The combination readily accepts touches of other brights.

WARM WITH EARTHY STRIPES

style
(6)
primer

Unleash the creativity of color with painted wall stripes. For a rich palette, work in earthy and coppery shades that impart a sense of traditional warmth. Terra-cotta, green, and yellow tones blend together beautifully.

PROPORTION & SCALE

designing with an eye to proportion and scale starts with understanding the terms. Proportion is the size of one part to the whole. Scale refers to dimensions of a piece in relation to the height and area in which it is placed—or to other pieces in the grouping. In practical terms, think of proportion relating to specific pieces of furniture. Are the legs of a table a pleasing height and circumference? Consider scale in choosing furnishings to work together. A large, high-back sofa needs chairs of similar size and weight. To avoid creating miniatures for adults, designers often reduce the number of pieces in a room, rather than the scale. A trend to fewer and larger pieces, sometimes frankly overscaled, is also seen in accessories. One bowl takes the place of myriad tiny objects on a table.

ANCHOR AND BALANCE

First rule: Choose furniture in scale with the room—the higher the ceiling, the taller and wider the anchoring pieces. Here, the curved height of the armoire is well above the top of the paneling to avoid blank wall space.

style
1
primer

style
②
primer

Designers create rooms of strong visual impact with a minimum number of maximum-size accessories. Larger pieces, such as this clock and hanging lantern, appear more visually important than groups of small objects.

OVERSCALE FOR IMPACT

PLEASURE OF PROPORTION

The upholstered bench demonstrates the importance of thoughtful design. Arms are gently curved and padded—for a look of ease that doesn't overwhelm the piece. Curved lines repeat in the neckroll pillow and ottoman.

style
③
primer

FURNITURE & FLOOR PLANS

lan how you are going to use a room before you purchase the major pieces. This rough idea will help you set priorities when you shop for the pieces that make a room work for you. If your living room is going to become a library or game room, consider the versatility of a pair or grouping of club chairs instead of a standard sofa. If your room is an odd shape or long and narrow, one of the newer, stylish sectional sofas or two loveseats may work best. Choose such major pieces with care and go with the more basic and tailored, such as solid or discreetly patterned fabrics. Remember this: For the money you would spend on new furniture, buy well-made secondhand furniture. Odds are they will be sturdier and better made. (The downside: having to eventually replace fabrics on upholstered pieces.)

MIX, DON'T MATCH

Gone are the days of purchasing matched furniture sets. Instead, style-conscious decorators mix chair styles and materials for personal (and affordable) decorating. One wonderful fabric works wonders for the final lively touch.

style
①
primer

Consignment and thrift shops offer some of the best buys in decorating—if you can overlook dated fabrics. If a piece is in good structural condition, shop for a youthful, colorful fabric. Re-cover in upbeat prints and contrasting patterns.

RESTYLE THRIFTY FINDS

ONE-OF-A-KIND CHAIRS

Take the guesswork out of pairing disparate chairs. Forget matching, but choose chairs of roughly the same height and width. Note the arm heights are similar here. A table, of matching arm height, bridges the gap between pieces.

FURNITURE & FLOOR PLANS

Work with your space and specific needs for the most functional furniture arrangement. In an open plan, place furniture, anchored by a rug, for a sitting area. Choose a dining table and chair size to comfortably fit your room.

style **5** primer

DIVIDE AND CONQUER

RETHINK YOUR BACKDROPS

style **4** primer

A large bed for a small room challenges creativity. Face the issue: Consider an unconventional arrangement such as backing the bed between windows and facing it into the room. Small tables complete the chic setting.

ARRANGED FOR TV AND TALK

style ⑥ primer

Tried-and-true arrangements—such as sofa plus two club chairs plus coffee table—are often the way to go. For comfortable viewing, place the sofa facing the television. Add chairs that turn in for conversation or out for viewing.

ART & ARRANGING

Savvy decorators know the secrets of selecting and arranging art. You don't need a large bank account or access to high-price galleries for wonderful pieces. Sources of intriguing art are diverse and ever-growing: local artist cooperatives, college and art school student and faculty sales, and reproduction prints of archival photography. Thrift stores and flea markets also carry prints and charming paintings whose personalities exceed humble origins. Display need not be prescriptive. Leave old paintings unframed to relax traditional art. Or mat and frame prints or photographs identically to arrange in a neat grid pattern. Paint unmatched frames linen white or a pale tint for a cottage or country look, or choose black frames and white mats to pull together a contemporary wall grouping.

STRENGTH OF SYMMETRY

For a symmetrical arrangement with a twist, stack four identically framed and matted prints between candestick lamps. Loosen the arrangement by hanging three artifacts above. Center an object, such as the box, on the table.

style

primer

Arrange odd numbers symmetrically for an ordered approach to displaying diverse objects. Repeating the horizontal line of the decorative headboard, two sets of prints flank a wreath with three plates centered above.

ODD NUMBERS WIN OUT

LEANING AND LAPPING

Hang picture shelves (an odd number is visually pleasing) to organize framed and matted black-and-white photographs. Lean and overlap prints to avoid blanks; fill in with edited accessories in contemporary shapes.

ART & ARRANGING

Vary shapes and sizes of the same type and same color of object (here floral tole trays) for a strong focal point. Center the largest object to anchor the easy arrangement. Flank with a pair or balanced grouping of similar objects.

style
⑤
primer

WEIGHED WITH BLACK TRAYS

ORDER FROM DIVERSITY

style
④
primer

Turn assorted prints, photographs, and frames into an arrangement with paint and mats. Work out the grouping on the floor or trace shapes on kraft paper and tape to the wall before nailing. Start in the center and work out.

FRAME WITH WATERCOLORS

Relax traditional art with innovative display. Here the two lower watercolor prints hang with the frame edges under the prints (inside the mats). The arrangement calls attention to the glazed, classical-style head plaque.

PATTERN & FABRIC

Pattern and fabric are the instant style-makers of decorating. A change in draperies, slip-covers, and wallpaper transforms the style, palette, and mood of a room—from English Country to Country French to Scandinavian. Fabrics and wall-papers with obvious patterns and vibrant color energize any room. Think of the combination of pattern and color like this: The more of both you have in a room, the livelier the mix will be. For harmony in such colorful settings, decorators choose a dominant pattern, in the largest scale, and work from it. Supporting fabrics and patterns repeat at least one of the colors in the dominant fabric—unless they are used as tiny accents. For pattern in a more edited scheme, classics such as blue and white, mix in various combinations of color values and patterns.

NEUTRAL PLUS PATTERN

Start with a neutral color, solid sofa for decorating options. Here, for an exotic mood, a colorful kilim enriches with pattern and sets the color scheme of rich, warm hues. A mix of plaids, checks, and solids energizes the setting.

style **①** primer

Concentrate pattern in lively, fresh colors. Small amounts of pattern are effective against a white background when color and pattern create a definite mood. Here, the lavender and green florals and plaids freshen the scene.

WHEN A LITTLE DOES A LOT

TWICE THE TOILE

Lovers of toile de Jouy never get enough of the French-style scenic prints. Designers like to use matching toile in mass quantity for impact. Loosen the traditional look by introducing a toile accent in a different color and design.

PATTERN & FABRIC

SOFTEN WITH SHEERS

ANCHORED BY WHITE

style
④
primer

Create a pretty, old-fashioned scheme with patterned blue-and-white wallpaper and draperies. Keep the room fresh and fun with white furniture and white linens. Edit bright accents to inexpensive, easy-to-change touches.

SHEERS PLUS PATTERN

Sheers are keeping up with the times. Patterned with color, such as the airy windowpane bed hanging, or pastel-colored, sheers are designer favorites. They mix well with florals and plaids that repeat the color accents.

accessories and collections are the fun touches of decorating. Favorite objects from near and far stamp your personality and sensibilities on your rooms. If you are already an avid collector, consider how to incorporate your collections or collectibles into your scheme. Whatever you collect—from refined tiny French porcelains to rusty hose nozzles—is fair game. Collections look more important when they are grouped together. Vary the heights of similar objects on stands or on stacked books for interest and as focal points. If you prefer a pared-down look, use favorite objects as the finishing touches to your rooms. The trend is to larger and fewer objects. A wood or pottery bowl from a gallery or crafts fair is stunning alone or grouped with stacked books on a coffee table or console.

BEST OF BUILT-INS

Serious collectors quickly run out of table and wall space. When space is tight, shelves can be designed to complement major furniture pieces and art. Attractive built-ins feature well-edited groupings of similar objects.

style
(1)
primer

Create a dramatic backdrop by combining curved glass shelves with standard painted plywood built-ins. Note the shelves feature an asymmetrical shelf grouping within the symmetrical wall unit—and wall-hung etchings.

CONTEMPORARY COLLECTOR

NEW AMERICAN COUNTRY

Painted folk art stands out against rich wall color. Here, the painted decorative chest is an art piece in its own right and a striking display for the model of Mount Vernon. Simplicity strengthens the charming setting.

LIGHTING & LAMPS

balanced lighting brings your rooms to life, creating mood and enhancing architectural features and artwork. For a starting point, decide whether the room needs overhead or specific task lighting. Dining rooms and dining areas traditionally use overhead sources. Consider chandelier, pendant, or other hanging fixtures; or look into contemporary styles—or an arrangement of two or more recessed lights. Dimmers, also called rheostats, are used to control lighting for atmosphere. For clear, white light, designers recommend low-voltage halogen lighting for recessed fixtures. Directional spot lighting calls attention to artwork while wall washers highlight textures or finishes. Balance overhead lighting with sconces, wall-mounted, swing-arm lamps, floor lamps, and table lamps.

CONTEMPORARY TIMES TWO

A combination of contemporary pendant and halogen fixtures turns a dining room into a gallery for abstract art. Lighting supply firms are sources for styles that pair with clean-lined furniture, bold colors, and abstract art.

style

primer

Purchase or make candlestick lamps in pairs with the base two-thirds of the total height; the "candle" and shade are pleasing as one-third. Arrange on a sideboard or console to flank a framed mirror or large painting.

CLASSIC CANDLESTICKS

STYLE-MAKING CHANDELIER

Err on the size of large if you are buying a reproduction or antique chandelier. Scale makes the focal fixture more important. Designers suggest hanging a chandelier so the bottom is about 30 inches above the top of the table.

LIGHTING & LAMPS

Introduce an element of the unexpected to a cottage or country room with a contemporary metal lamp. You'll find these widely reproduced, desk-type lamps feature movable arms that easily adjust for comfortable reading.

style
5
primer

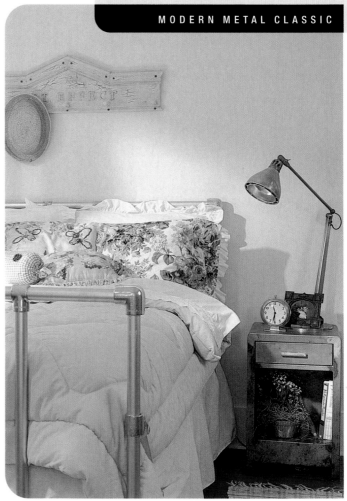

MODERN METAL CLASSIC

BARLEY TWIST AND BLACK

style
4
primer

A quality classic lamp is an investment piece that spans years and decorating styles—the classic shapes and materials don't quickly date. Here, the linen shade adds a fashionable touch of black to a traditional living room.

DRESS UP SWING-ARMS

style
⑥
primer

Think outside the bedroom for uses of swing-arm lamps. Add stylish, correct size shades (here covered to match faux leopard pillows) and three-way light bulbs to create reading nooks wherever you enjoy reading or relaxing.

STORARGE & DISPLAY

W hat is storage and what is display comes down to a fine line, often crossed in decorating. With attractive open shelves and neat arrangements, even utilitarian items contribute to a chic decorating scheme. In kitchens, designers use open shelving for dishes, glassware, and bowls; pegboard and racks organize tools and pots and pans. Baskets and bins provide concealed storage in such open arrangements. This mix of open and concealed storage and display is also the design direction for home offices and living and family room built-ins. With an ever-increasing number of attractive storage products from specialty and discount stores, it's easy to find boxes, bins, and containers for the clutter you want to conceal. Repurpose baskets and wood or metal boxes of all shapes and sizes.

HANDY AND STYLISH

Organize open storage with matching metal record bins—available from shops and catalogs that specialize in storage solutions and from some discount stores. Add flat attaché cases or hampers for extra concealed storage.

style
1
primer

style
②
primer

Color code open storage by painting the interiors of cube-style shelving in a mix of your favorite vibrant colors. Add plastic bins and boxes—and a painted flowerpot or two for pencils and pens—to organize your office supplies.

BRIGHT IS RIGHT

OPEN AND CLOSED STORAGE

When you need a lot of storage, include a solid wall of built-ins. Tricks to style: vary the heights of the shelves (or install on adjustable tracks), include concealed storage, group like objects, and arrange without overcrowding.

style
③
primer

SHOPS OF INTEREST

ALABAMA SHOPS

The Rerun Shop, 2209 3rd Ave. North, Birmingham, Alabama 35203, 205/328-3602

Tricia's Treasures, 1433-5 Montgomery Hwy., Vestavia, AL 35216, 205/822-0004

Neat Stuff, 205 Linden St., Trussville, AL 35173, 205/655-0255

On a Shoestring, 601 Shades Crest Rd., Hoover, AL 35226, 205/822-8741

The Garage, 2304 10th Terrace S., Birmingham, AL 35205, 205/254-9018

ARKANSAS SHOPS

Cabbage Rose, 5701 Kavanaugh, Little Rock, AR 72207, 501/664-4042

Fabulous Finds Antique Mall, 1521 Merrill Dr., Little Rock, AR 72211, 501/224-6622

Pflugrad's Antiques, 5624 R St., Little Rock, AR 72207, 501/661-0188

Marshall Clements Interiors, Inc., 1509 Rebsamen Park Rd., Little Rock, AR 72202, 501/663-1828, fax: 501/663-6366, MarshallClements@aol.com

CALIFORNIA SHOPS

Fat Chance, 162 N. La Brea Ave., Los Angeles, CA 90036, 323/930-1960

Futurama, 446 N. La Brea Ave., Los Angeles, CA 90036, 323/937-4522

Modernica, 7360 Beverly Blvd., Los Angeles, CA 90036, 323/933-0383

The Fainting Couch, 7405 Beverly Blvd., Los Angeles, CA 90036, 323/930-0106

Soolip Bungalow, 548 Norwian Dr., Los Angeles, CA 90048, 310/360-1512

Plastica, 685 Hollywood Blvd., Los Angeles, CA 90027, 323/644-1212

Plastica, 8405 3rd St., Los Angeles, CA 90048, 323/644-1212, www.plastica.org,

Son Antiques, 7912 Melrose Ave., Los Angeles, CA 90048, 323/651-0521

Blueprint, 8366 Beverly Blvd., Los Angeles, CA 90048, 213/653-2439

Shelter, 7920 Beverly Bvd., Los Angeles, CA 90048, 323/937-3222

Off the Wall, 816 N. La Cienega Blvd., Los Angeles, CA 90069

And, 7325 Melrose Ave., Los Angeles, CA 90046, 323/930-1185

Algabar, 920 N. La Cienega Blvd., Los Angeles, CA 90036, 323/360-3500

Emmerson Troop Furniture, 7957 Melrose Ave., West Hollywood, CA 90046, 323/635-9763

Pom Pom, 6819 Melrose Ave., Los Angeles, CA 90038, 323/938-6286, fax: 323/938-1820

Pom Pom, 326 N. La Brea Ave., Los Angeles, CA 90036, 323/934-2051, fax: 323/934-2986

Pom Pom the Garden Room, 7169 Beverly Blvd., Los Angeles, CA 90036, 323/936-2022

Macy's Furniture Outlet, 3880 N. Mission, Los Angeles, CA 90031, 323/227-2662

Country Downs Interiors, 1302 Camino del Mar, Del Mar, CA 92014, 858/481-1356

Circa a.d., 3867 4th Ave., San Diego, CA 92103, 619/293-3328, info@circaad.com, www.circaad.com

Dupuis, 1555 Camino del Mar, Del Mar, CA 92014, 619/793-0109

Metropolis, 1003 University Ave., San Diego, CA 92103, 619/220-0632

Mermaids, 7441 Girard Ave., La Jolla, CA 92037, 619/220-0632

Antique Warehouse, 212 S. Cedros, Solana Beach, CA 92075, 858/755-5156

Cedros Trading Co., 307 S. Cedros Ave., Solana Beach, CA 92075, 619/794-9016

Cedros Gardens, 330 S. Cedros, Solana Beach, CA 92075, 619/792-8640

Bazaar del Mundo, 2754 Calhoun, San Diego, CA 92110, 619/296-3161

Bo Danica, 7722 Girard Ave., La Jolla, CA 92037, 619/454-6107

Outrageous Rugs, 7126 Miramar Road, San Diego, CA 92121, 619/536-9118

Silver Skillet, 2690 Via De La Valle, Del Mar, CA 92014, 619/481-6710

Architectural Salvage, 1971 India St., San Diego, CA 92101, 619/696-1313

King and Company, 7470 Girard Ave., La Jolla, CA 92037, 619/454-1504

Birdcage, 143 S. Cedros Ave., Solana Beach, CA 92075, 858/793-6262

Island Provenance, 1053 B Ave., Coronado, CA 92118, 619/435-8232

Girard Avenue Collection, 7505 Girard Ave., La Jolla, CA 92037, 858/459-7765, www.girardantiques.com

Vintage Rose, 24 S. Cedros Ave., Solana Beach, CA 92075, 619/796-1668

One Half, 1837 Polk St., San Francisco, CA 94109, 415/775-1416

Gift Outlet, 1455 East Francisco Blvd., San Rafael, CA 94901, 415/256-1884

Stonelight Tile Co. Showroom and Yard, 609 South First St., San Jose, CA 95113, 408/292-7424

House of Values, 2565 S. El Camino Real, San Mateo, CA 94403, 650/349-3420

Benicia Foundry & Iron Works, Inc., 2995 Bayshore Rd., Benicia, CA 94510, 707/745-4645, www.beniciafoundry.com

Iguana Ameramex, 301 Jefferson St., Oakland, CA 94607, 510/834-5848 www.iguana-mexico.com

Tradeway Stores, 10860 San Pablo Ave., El Cerrito, CA 94530, 510/529-2360

The Wooden Duck, 2919 7th St., Berkeley, CA 94710, 510/848-3575, fax: 510/848-3512, www.thewoodenduck.com

Building Resources, 701 Amador St., San Francisco, CA 94124, 415/285-7814

Caldwell Building Wreckers, 195 Bayshore Blvd., San Francisco, CA 94124, 415/550-6777

San Francisco Museum of Modern Art Rental Gallery, Building A, Fort Mason Center, San Francisco, CA 94123, 415/441-4777

Pioneer Home Supply, 657 Mission St., 5th Floor, San Francisco, CA 94105, 415/543-1234

Roger's Gardens, 2301 San Joaquin Hills Rd., Corona Del Mar, CA 92625, 949/640-5800

Santa Monica Antique Market, 1607 Lincoln Blvd., Santa Monica, CA 90404, 310/314-4899

Little Folk Art, 1120 Montana Ave., Santa Monica, CA 90403, 310/576-0909

Subtle Tones, 844 Avocado, Newport Beach, CA 92660, 949/640-2781

The Blue House, 1402 Montana Ave., Santa Monica, CA 90403, 310/451-2243

Bountiful, 1335 Abbot Kinney Blvd., Venice, CA 90291, 310/450-3620

Room With a View, 1600 Montana Ave., Santa Monica, CA 90403, 310/998-5858, RoomView.com

Nicholson's Antiques, 362 N. Coast Hwy., Laguna Beach, CA 92651, 949/494-4820

Jefferies Ltd., 852 Production Pl., Newport Beach, CA 92663, 949/642-4154

Richard Gould Antiques, 808 N. La Cienega Blvd., Los Angeles, CA 90069, 310/657-9416

Hollyhock, 214 North Larchmont Blvd., Los Angeles, CA 90004, 323/931-3400

Geary's Beverly Hills, 351 North Beverly Dr., Beverly Hills, CA 90210, 310/273-4741

Tirage Art, 1 West California Blvd., Pasadena, CA 91105, 818/952-1028

Palazzetti, 9006 Beverly Blvd., Los Angeles, CA 90048, 310/273-2225

City Antiques, 8444 Melrose Ave., Los Angeles, CA 90069, 323/658-6354

Bruce Graney & Co., 1 West California Blvd., Pasadena, CA 91105, 626/449-9547, bruce@brucegraneyantiques.com

Shelter, 7920 Beverly Blvd., Los Angeles, CA 90048, 323/937-3222

Rubbish Interiors, 1630 Silverlake Blvd., Silverlake, CA 90026, 323/661-5575.

Off the Wall, 816 N. La Cienega Blvd., Los Angeles, CA 90069, 310/360-1080

Emmerson Troop Furniture, 7957 Melrose Ave., West Hollywood, CA 90046, 323/653-9763

Steelworks Design Studio and Gallery, 6604 San Pablo Ave., Oakland, CA 94608

CONNECTICUT SHOPS

Braswell Galleries, 125 West Avenue, Norwalk, CT 06854, 203/899-7420

design solutions, 146 Elm Street, New Canaan, CT 06840, 203/966-3116

Design Store at the Door Store, 195 Greenwich Avenue, Greenwich, CT 06830, 203/861-7565

Lillian August, 289 Greenwich Avenue, Greenwich, CT 06830, 203/629-1539

Lillian August, 17 Main Street, Westport, CT 06880, 203/454-1775

Lillian August wareHouse, 85 Water Street, South Norwalk, CT 06854

Scofield Furniture Store, 130 Main Street, New Canaan, CT 06840, 203/966-0136

Silvermine Guild of Art, 1037 Silvermine Road, New Canaan, CT 06840, 203/866-0411,

FLORIDA SHOPS

Arango, 7519 Dadeland Mall, Miami, FL 33156,

305/661-4229

Details at Home, 1711 Alton Road, Miami Beach, FL 33139, 305/531-1325, fax: 305/674-0135 www.detailsathome.com, and, 1542 S. Dixie Hwy.,Coral Gables, FL 33146, 305/669-3815; fax: 305/669-3825

Now, A Style Store, 51 NE 40th St., Miami, FL 33139, 305/573-9988; fax:305/573-9909 fax: 305/573-9909

Orson, 74 NE 40th St., Miami, FL 33137, 305/573-6805

Room, 99 NE 39t St., Miami, FL 33137, 305/438-1966, call 188/420-7666 for catalog

World Resources, 56 NE 40th St., Miami, FL 33137, 305/576-8799, toll free: 877/576-8799, www.worldresources.com

GEORGIA SHOPS

Gado Gado, 549 Amsterdam, Atlanta, GA 30306, 404/885-1818

Provenance, 1145 Foster, Atlanta, GA 30318, 404/351-1217

Innovations, 1011 Monroe Dr. NE, Atlanta, GA 30306, 404/881-8111

The Curtain Exchange, 1183 Howell Mill Road, Atlanta, GA 30318, 404/352-8849

Previews Interiors & Antiques, 4524 Forsythe Rd., Macon, GA 31210, 800/456-1086

ILLINOIS SHOPS

Pavilion, 1812 N. Milwaukee Ave., Chicago, IL 60647-4411

Yardifacts, 1864 N. Damen, Chicago, IL 60647, 773/342-9273

Pagoda Red, 1714 N. Damen, Chicago, IL 60647, 773/235-1188, www.pagodared.com,

Embelezar, 1639 N. Damen, Chicago, IL 60647, 773/645-9705

Jayson Home & Garden, 1911 N. Clybourn, Chicago, IL 60614, 773/525-3100

The Morton Collection, 100 E. Walton, Chicago, IL 60611, 312/587-7400

Elements, 102 E. Oak, Chicago, IL 60611, 312/642-6574

Tabula Tua, 1015 W. Armitage, Chicago, IL 60614, 773/525-3500

Faded Rose, 1017 W. Armitage, Chicago, IL 60614, 773/281-8161, fax: 773/281-9301

Fortunate Discoveries, 1022 W. Armitage, Chicago, IL 60614, 773/404-0212

Ancient Echoes, 1003 W. Armitage, Chicago, IL 60614, 773/880-1003

Findables, 907 W. Armitage, Chicago, IL 60614, 773/348-0674

Art Effect, 651 W. Armitage, Chicago, IL 60614, 312/664-0997, arteffectchicago.com

Jean Alan, 2134 N. Damen, Chicago, IL 60647, 773/278-2345; fax 773/278-2389

Whizbang, 2117 N. Damen, Chicago, IL 60647, 773/292-9602, www.whizbang.qpg.com

Chiasso, Water Tower Place, 835 N. Michigan Ave., Level 2, Chicago, IL 60611, 312/280-1249

Eclectic Junction for Art, 1630 N. Damen, Chicago, IL 60647, 773/342-7865

Home Climate, 2462 N. Clark, Chicago, IL 60614, 773/327-7717; fax 773/327-7759

IOWA SHOPS

Main Street Antiques and Art, 110 W. Main St., Box 340, West Branch, IA 52358, 319/643-2065, e mail: msantiques@bigplanet.com

Ames Greenhouse and Floral, 3011 S. Duff Ave., Ames, IA 50010, 515/232-1332, 800/340-1332

The Callanan Collection Estate & Consignment Sales, 2122 Grand Ave., Des Moines, IA 50312, 515/243-2124

KANSAS SHOPS

FOB Kansas City, 9024 Metcalf Avenue, Overland Park, KS 66212, 913/381-8910

Tuesday Mornings Rug Outlet, 5320 Martway, Mission, KS 66205, 913/671-7175

Vintage Boutique, 2360 N. Maize Rd., Wichita, KS 67205, 316/729-1972

KENTUCKY SHOPS

Meridian, 4660 Shelbyville Road, Louisville, KY 40207, 502/895-3151

MAINE SHOPS

Wells Union, 1755 Post Road, Wells, ME 04090, 207/646-6130

Antiques USA, U.S. Coastal Route 1, Kennebunk, ME 04043, 207/985-7766, e mail: antiqusa@aol.com

MARYLAND SHOPS

Edward & Edward, 35 S. Carroll St., Fredrick, MD 21701, 301/695-9674

Ancient Rhythms, 7920 Woodmont Ave., Bethesda, MD 20814, 301/652-2669, www.ancientrhythms.com

Great Finds & Design, 1925 Greenspring Drive,

Timonium, MD 21093, 410/561-9413

Terra Cognita, 7920 Norfolk Ave., Bethesda, MD 20814, 301/907-3055, fax: 301/907/2434

MICHIGAN SHOPS

Lovell & Whyte, 14950 Lakeside Road, Lakeside MI 49116, 616/469-5900

The Plum Tree, 16337 Red Arrow Hwy., Union Pier, MI 49129, 616/469-5980

MINNESOTA SHOPS

Stick & Stones, Ltd., 2914 Hennepin Ave. S., St. Paul, MN 55408, 612/827-6121

Spare Room., 2817 Hennepin Ave., Minneapolis, MN 55408, 612/870-0887

Spare Room, 1705 North Snelling, St. Paul, MN 55118, 651/645-3973

Depth of Field, 405 Cedar, Minneapolis, MN 55454, 612/339-6061

Depth of Field, 917 Grand Avenue, St. Paul, MN 55105, 651/222-5356

Depth of Field, 7433 France Avenue, Edina, MN 55435, 612/835-4606

Dean Gallery, 2815 South Hennepin Avenue, Minneapolis, MN 55408, 612/872-4976

Crescent Moon, 58 S. Hamline, St. Paul, MN 55105, 651/690-9630

Grand Addictions, 1460 Grand Avenue, St. Paul, MN 55105, 651/698-6777

Home at Last, Town Center Mall, 41st Ave. & Hwy. 81, Robbinsdale, MN 55422, 612/533-8287

Elements, 2940 W. 66th St., Richfield, MN 55423, 612/866-0631

Go Home, 1408 W. Lake, Minneapolis, MN 55408, 612/824-8732

Plaza Antiques, 1758 Hennepin Ave., Minneapolis, MN 55403-2121, 612/377-7331

Mary O'Neal & Co., 221 Water St., Excelsior, MN 55331, 612/470-0205, 612/473-1554

Corner Door Inc., 1250 E. Wayzata Blvd., Wayzata, MN 55391, 612/473-2274

etc, 2, 850 East Lake St., Wayzata, MN 55391, 612/473-1435

Paris Flea Market, 5005 France Ave. S. Edina, MN 55410, 612/928-9923

Bella Galleria, 1338 Randolph Ave., St. Paul, MN 55104, 651/698-8662

Weasel Pop, 244 S. Albert St., St. Paul, MN 55105, 651/699-6556, hnomad@hotmail.com

Designer Marketplace at K.D.S., 241 Freemont Ave. N. (off Glenwood Ave.), Minneapolis, MN 55405, 612/381-8508

Minneapolis College of Art and Design MCAD, 2501 Stevens Ave. S., Minneapolis, MN 55404-4347, 612/874-3790, (annual December sale)

MISSOURI SHOPS

Décor Upholstery, 7110 McGee, Kansas City, MO 64114, 816/363-3140

Cheep Antiques, 500 W. 5th St., Kansas City, MO 64105, 816/471-0092

Factory Outlet Eddie Bauer, 2035 Independence Center Dr., Independence, MO 64057, 816/795-9211

Boomerang, 1415 W. 39th St., Kansas City, MO 64111, 816/531-6111, kjkboomer1@aol.com

NEW YORK SHOPS

Blue Moon Antiques, 219 Broadway, Saratoga Springs, NY 12866, 518/580-0032

Regent Street Antique Center, 153 Regent St., Saratoga Springs, NY 12866, 518/584-0107

Armory Antiques, P.O. Box 352, Hudson, NY 12534, 518/822-1477, www.armoryantiques.com

New York Central II, Inc. Framing and Furniture Annex, 102 Third Avenue, 12th & 3rd St., New York, NY 10003, 212/420-6060

Door Store...your design store, 1 Park Ave., New York, NY, 10016, 212/679-9700, fax: 212/685-9386, www.doorstorefurniture.com 1 Park Avenue at 33rd Street, New York, NY 10016

Design Store at the Door Store, 1201 Third Avenue at 70th Street, New York, NY 10021

Design Store at the Door Store, 123 West 17th Street, New York, NY 10011

Design Store at the Door Store, 67 Old County Road, Carl Place, Long Island, NY

Rustika, 63 Crosby St., New York, NY 10012, 212/965-0004

Bittersweet Interiors, 110 Greene St., New York, NY 10012, 212/343-2322

Country Home & Comfort, 835 Broadway, New York, NY 10003, 212/254-8920; fax: 212/254-8136

Uproar Home Furnishings, 121 Greene St., New York, NY 10021, 212/614-8580

Portico Bed and Bath, 139 Spring St., New York, NY 10012, 214/941-7722

Trailer Park, 77 Sterling Place, Brooklyn, NY 11217, 718/623-2170

Olde Good Things, 400 Atlantic Ave., Brooklyn, NY 11217, 718/935-9742

Olde Good Things, 124 West 46th St., New York, NY 10011, 212/246-1129; 888/551-7333, e-mail: info@oldegoodthings.com; website: www.oldegoodthings.com

The Attic, 220 Court Street, Brooklyn, NY 11231, 718/643-9535

Granny's Attic, 305 Smith St., Brooklyn, NY 11231, 718/624-0175

NORTH CAROLINA SHOPS

Graphik Dimensions Ltd. (mail order), 2103 Brentwood St., High Point, NC 27263, 800/221-0262, www.pictureframes.com

Blacklion, 10605 Park Road, Charlotte, NC 28210, 704/541-1148

Blacklion, 20601 Torrence Chapel Road, Cornelius, NC 28031, 704/895-9539

Blacklion, 8261 Concord Mills Blvd., Concord, NC 28027, 704/979-5466

Eclectix—The Best of Home Styles, 2102 South Blvd., Suite 100, Charlotte, NC 28203, 704/376-0575, www.eclectix.com

Ciel Home, 601 Providence Road, Charlotte, NC 28207, 704/372-3335

Porter and Prince, 51 Thompson St., Suite E, Asheville, NC 28803, 828/236-2337

The Loft, 53 Broadway, Asheville, NC 28801 828/259-9303, loftmax@cs.com

The Gardener's Cottage, 34 All Souls Crescent, Asheville, NC 28803, 828/277-2020

Interiors Marketplace, 2 Hendersonville Rd., Asheville, NC 28803, 828/253-2300

The Gardener's Cottage, S. Main St., Saluda, NC 28773, 828/749-4200

The Brass Latch, S. Main St., Saluda, NC 28773, 828/749-4200

OKLAHOMA SHOPS

England & Harp, 1515 E. 15th St., Tulsa, OK 74120, 918/582-3299

PENNSYLVANIA SHOPS

Olde Good Things, 450 Gilligan St. (warehouse), Scranton, PA 18508, 570/341-7668

SOUTH CAROLINA

GDC, 975 Savannah Highway, Charleston, SC 29401, 800/571-5142

TENNESSEE SHOPS

Meridian, 2711 Franklin Pike, Nashville,
TN 37204, 615/463-0555, www.meridian.com

The Iron Gate, 919 Columbia Ave., Franklin,
TN 37064, 615/791-7511

Savannah West, 343 Main St., Franklin, TN
37064, 615/791-0159

TEXAS SHOPS

August Antiques, 803 Heights Blvd., Houston,
TX 77007, 713/880-3353

Surroundings, 1710 Sunset Blvd., Houston,
TX 77005, 713/527-9838

Junque, 2303 Dunlavy at Maryland, Houston,
TX 77006, 713/529-2177

Flashback Funtiques, 1627 Westheimer,
Houston, TX 77006, 713/522-7900

Happy's Furnishings, 114 West Main,
Waxahachie, TX 75165, 972/937-6767

The Front Desk, 10401 Harry Hines, Dallas,
TX 75220, 214/904-9045 or 800/299-8095,
e-mail: johncrisford@airmail.net

Rutherfords, 5647 West Lovers Lane, Dallas,
TX 75209, 214/357-0888

GSD&M Idea City, Prison Art Auction, 828 W. 6th,
Austin, TX 78703, 512/459-5490

Aqua 20th Century Modern, 1415 S. Congress
Ave., Austin, TX 78704, 512/916-8800;
www.aquamodern.com

Uncommon Objects, 1512 S. Congress Ave.,
Austin, TX 78704, 512/442-4000

Point Five, 2444 Times Blvd., Suite 100A,
Houston, TX 77005, 713/529-5550

Uncommon Market, 2701 Fairmount, Dallas,
TX 75201, 214/871-2775

Interior Alternative, 1305 Inwood Rd., Dallas,
TX 75247, 214/637-8800

Debris, 1205 Slocum St., Dallas, TX 75207,
214/752-8855, debrisantiques@msn.com

The Mews, 1708 Market Center Blvd., Dallas,
TX 75247, 214/748-9070

Lots of Furniture Warehouse, 910 N. Industrial
Blvd., Dallas, TX 75247, 214/761-1575

Bab's Rue De Brocante Antiques, 2772 N.
Henderson, Dallas, TX 75206, 214/887-0070

Collage 20th Century Classics,
2820 N. Henderson Ave., Dallas, TX 75206,
214/828-9888

Vertu, 4514 Travis St., Suite 125, Dallas,
TX 75205, 214/520-7817

Roth and Schuster, 4514 Travis St., Suite 101,
Dallas, TX 75205, 214/528-1347

Green & Garzotto at Home, 4445 Travis St.,
Shop 101, Dallas, TX 75205, 214/528-0040,
www.greengarzotoathome.com,
paul@greengarzottoathome.com

Emeralds to Coconuts, 2730 N. Henderson Ave.,
Dallas, TX 75206, 214/823-3620

VIRGINIA SHOPS

Cielo Antiques & Accessories, 102 N. Fayette
St., Alexandria, VA 22314, 703/684-6722
websites: estatestuff.com; cieloantiques.com

C. Schuyler, Inc., 1218 King St., Alexandria,
VA 22314, 703/519/9490

Green Front, 316 S. Main St., Farmville,
VA 23901, 804/392-4912

WASHINGTON SHOPS

Watson Kennedy Fine Living, 86 Pine St.,
Seattle, WA 98101, 206/617-9678

WASHINGTON D.C. SHOPS

Ruff & Ready Furnishings, 1908 14th St. NW,
Washington, D.C. 20009, 202/667-7833

Millenium Decorative Arts, 1528 U St. NW,
Washington, D.C. 20009, 202/483-1218

Good Wood Inc., 1428 U St. NW,
Washington, D.C. 20009, 202/986-3640

CONSIGNMENT/OUTLETS

ALABAMA CONSIGNMENTS

Estate Sales Store and Consignment, 4244
Cahaba Heights Ct., Birmingham, AL 35243,
205/969-0904

B & B Outlet, 6th St., Hwy. 231 S., Oneonta,
AL 35121, 205/274-2219; fax 205/274-2288

CALIFORNIA CONSIGNMENTS

Marin General Hospital Thrift Shop, 1328 Fourth
Street, San Rafael, CA 94901, 415/456-1430

UCLA Medical Center Auxiliary Thrift Shop,
11271 Massachusetts Avenue, Los Angeles,
CA 90025, 310/478-1793

Children's Hospital & Health Thrift Shop,
3590 5th Avenue, San Diego, CA 92103

Next-To-New Shop, 2226 Fillmore Street,
San Francisco, CA 94115

Village Consignment, 1150 Camino Del, Del Mar,
CA 92014, 619/259-0870

Art Exchange, 77 Geary Blvd., 2nd Floor,

San Francisco, CA 94108, 415/956-5750

Macy's Furniture Clearance Center, 1208
Whipple Rd., Union City, CA 9458, 510/441-8833

National Furniture Liquidators, 845
Embarcadero, Oakland, CA 94606, 510/251-2222

Lumber Liquidators, 1061 Eastshore Highway,
Albany, CA 94710, 510/524-7800

R. Elements Factory Outlet, 938 Tyler St., #104,
Benicia, CA 94510, 707/746-0235

Smith & Hawken Outlet, 1330 Tenth St.,
Berkeley, CA 94710

Judie Bomberger, Inc. Seconds Outlet,
65-J Hamilton Dr., Novato, CA 94949,
415/883-3072

Candle Outlet, 1223 Donnelly Ave., Burlingame,
CA 94010, 650/343-0804

Designers' Warehouse Sale, 414 Lesser St.,
Oakland, CA 94601, 510/434-1600

Furniture Mart Sample Sales,
1355 Market Street, San Francisco, CA 94103,
415/552-2311

Giftcenter Sample Sales, 888 Brannan Street,
San Francisco, CA 94103, 415/864-SALE,
e-mail: maxine.newman@excite.com

House of Values, 2565 S. El Camino Real, San
Mateo, CA 94403, 650/349-3414

COLORADO CONSIGNMENTS

The Second Time Shop, 351 West Grand,
Englewood, CO 80110, 303/789-4055

CONNECTICUT CONSIGNMENTS

Middlesex Hospital Auxiliary, 1234 Boston Post
Road, Old Saybrook, CT 06475, 860/388-9606

Hospital for Special Care Auxiliary Shop,
73 Arch Street, New Britain, CT 06051,
860/223-4788

University of Connecticut Health Center
Auxiliary, 270 Park Road, West Hartford,
CT 06119, 860/586-8047

Greenwich Hospital Thrift Shop, 9B Sherwood
Place, Greenwich, CT 06830, 203/869-6124

Rummage Room, 191 Sound Beach Avenue, Old
Greenwich, CT 06870, 203/637-1875

Darien Community Thrift Shop, 996 Post Road,
Darien, CT 06820, 203/655-4552

Merry Go Round, 38 Arch Street, Greenwich,
CT 06830, 203/869-3155,

Consign It, 115 Mason Street, Greenwich,
CT 06830, 203/869-9836

DELAWARE CONSIGNMENTS

The Interior Alternative, 1325 Cooches Bridge Rd., Newark, DE 19713, 302/454-3232

FLORIDA CONSIGNMENTS

ABC Carpet & Home Outlet, 777 S. Congress, Delray Beach, FL 33445, 561/279-7777

Estate Sales Center, 4211 Salzedo Ave., Coral Gables, FL 33146, 305/448-0768

Details at Home Outlet, 3227 NE 2nd Ave., Miami, FL 33137, 305/571-9055

Interiors on Consignment, 887 Donald Ross Road, Juno Beach, FL 33408, 561/622-4100, fax: 561/622-9853

Interiors on Consignment, 7600 S. Dixie Hwy., West Palm Beach, FL 33405, 561/533-1690, fax: 561/533-1631

True Treasures, Crystal Tree Center, 1201 U.S. Highway One, North Palm Beach, FL 33408, 561/625-9569

Consigned, 11141 U.S. Highway One, North Palm Beach, FL 33408, 561/622-4991

The Nearly New Shop, 2218 South Dixie Highway, West Palm, FL 33401, 561/655-2230

South End Estate Sales, 4800 S. Dixie Highway, West Palm Beach, FL 33405, 561/820-9655

The Church Mouse, Bethesda-by-the-Sea Resale Shop, 375 S. County Road, Palm Beach, FL 33480, 561/659-2154

Boca Bargoons, 910 Federal Hwy., North Palm Beach, FL 33408, 561/842-7444

Boca Bargoons, 190 NW 20th Street, Boca Raton, FL 33431, 561/842-7444, www.bocabargoons.com

Trim Endless, 176 NW 20th St, Boca Raton, FL 33431, 561/347-8880

GEORGIA CONSIGNMENTS

Ballard's Backroom, 1670 DeFoor Ave. NW, Atlanta, GA 30318, 404/352-2776

Ballard's Backroom, 1475 Holcomb Bridge Road, Atlanta, GA 30318, 770/594-0102

ILLINOIS CONSIGNMENTS

Children's White Elephant Shop, 2380 N. Lincoln Avenue, Chicago, IL 60614, 773/281-3747

Hidden Treasures, (benefits Northwestern Memorial Hospital), 46 E. Chicago Ave., Chicago, IL 60611, 312/943-7761

Mt. Sinai Hospital Resale, 814 West Diversey Parkway, Chicago, IL 60614, 773/935-1434

1st Chance Upscale Resale, 1799 St. Johns Avenue, Highland Park, IL 60035, 847/433-9490

Time after Time Resale Shop, 2027 W. North Ave., Chicago, IL 60647, 773/342-4323; fax: 773/342-4531

Pier One Imports Clearance Store, 780 Lakehurst Road, Waukegan, IL 60085 847/689-1121

Pier One, 4249 W. 211th, Matteson, IL 60443, 708/748-3525

The Haeger Potteries Outlet, 7 Maiden Lane (off Van Buren), East Dundee, IL 60118, 847/426-3441

1730 Outlet Company, 1730 W. Wrightwood, Chicago, IL 60614, 773/871-4331, www.1730 outlet.com

The Courtyard, 63 Village Place, Hinsdale, IL. 60521, 630/323-1135

P.O.S.H., 3729 N. Southport, Chicago, IL 60613, 773/529-7674, www.POSHCHICAGO.com

Consign Design, 1128 W. Armitage, Chicago, IL 60614, 773/388-2894

Elliott Consignment, 2465 N. Lincoln Ave., Chicago, IL 60614, 773/404-6080

Southport Antiques & Consignments, 3819 N. Southport, Chicago, IL 60613, 773/665-9650

Gabriel's Trumpet, 229 Rice Lake Square, Wheaton, IL 60187, 630-871-9500

Interiors on Consignment, 1809 W. Webster Ave., Chicago, IL 60614, 773/384-0769.

Time Well, 2780 N. Lincoln Ave., Chicago, IL 60614, 773/549-2113

LOUISIANA CONSIGNMENTS

The Curtain Exchange, 3947 Magazine St., New Orleans, LA 70115, 504/897-2444; and 3506 Magazine St., New Orleans, LA 70115, 504/269-9634; fax: 504/269-8488; thecurtainexchange.com

New Orleans Auction Galleries, 801 Magazine, New Orleans, LA 70130

MARYLAND CONSIGNMENTS

Select Seconds Hospital Thrift, 8 East Patrick Street, Frederick, MD 21701, 301/662-8280

MASSACHUSETTS CONSIGNMENTS

Friends Thrift Shop, (Beth Israel Deaconess Medical Center), 25 Harvard St., Brookline, MA 02146, 617/566-7016

Friends Thrift Shop, Corner of Pilgrim Road and Crossover Street, Boston, MA 02215, 617/632-8168

FriendShop/Flower Shop—East Campus, Beth Israel Deaconess Medical Center, 330 Brookline Ave., Stoneman Building, 2nd Floor, Boston, MA 02215, 617/667-3639

FriendShop/Flower Shop—West Campus, Beth Israel Deaconess Medical Center, 185 Pilgrim Road, Farr Building, Lobby, Boston, MA 02215, 617/632-8168

Upscale ConsignMINT, 560 Lincoln Street, Worcester, MA 01605, 508/852-2606

MINNESOTA CONSIGNMENTS

H & B Gallery, 2729 Hennepin Aven., Minneapolis, MN 55408, 612/874-6436; fax: 612/813/0602

Carrol Shepherd's Consignment Shop, 18285 Minnetonka Blvd., Deephaven, MN 55391

Main Street Consignment, 4605 Shady Oak Road, Hopkins, MN 55343, 612/933-9791

A Carousel Consignment Parlor, 735 N. Snelling Ave., Saint Paul, MN 55104, 612/699-5416

Architectural Antiques, 607 Washington Ave. S., Minneapolis, MN 55422, 612/332-8344, fax: 612/332-8967, www.archantiques.com; and 316 N. Main St., Stillwater, MN 55082, 651/439-2133

Legacy Architectural Salvage, Gallery of Minneapolis, 2101 Kennedy St. NE #190, Minneapolis, MN 55413, 612/378-3705, www.legacy-mpls.com, e-mail: info@legacy-mpls.com

Bauer Brothers Salvage, 2432 2nd St. N., Minneapolis, MN 55411, 612/331-9492

Dayton's Outlet Store, 701 Industrial Blvd., Minneapolis, MN 55413, 612/623-7111

Gabbert's Funiture, Odds and Ends Room, 3501 Galleria, Edina, MN 55435, 612/927-1500

Room & Board Outlet, 4680 Olson Memorial, Golden Valley, MN 55422, 612/529-6089

Baby + Teen Outlet, 5740 Wayzata Blvd., Golden Valley, MN 55422, 612/544-5422

Pine-Tique Furniture Company, Manufacturer Warehouse, 6022 Culligan Way, Minnetonka, MN 55345, 612/935-9595, www.pinetique.com

NEW YORK CONSIGNMENTS

Arthritis Foundation Thrift Shop Inc., 121 East 77th St., New York, NY 10021, 212/772-8816,

Calvary/St. George's Furniture Shop, 277 Park Avenue S, New York, NY 10010, 212/4756645

Parish of Calvary/St. George's, 61 Gramercy Park North, New York, NY 10010, 212/475-2674

City Opera Thrift Shop, 222 East 23rd Street, New York, NY 10010, 212/684-5344

Godmother's League Thrift Shop, 1459 Third Avenue, New York, NY 10028, 212/988-2858

Housing Works Thrift Shop, 143 West 17th Street, New York, NY 10011, 212/366-0820

Housing Works Thrift Shop, 202 East 77th Street, New York, NY 10021, 212/772-8461

Housing Works Thrift Shop, 306 Columbus Ave., New York, NY 10023, 212/579-7566

Memorial Sloan-Kettering Cancer Center Thrift Shop, 1440 Third Avenue at 82nd Street, New York, NY 10028, 212/535-1250

Cancer Care Thrift Shop, 1480 Third Avenue, New York, NY 10028, 212/879-9868

On Consignment, 17 Pondfield Road, Bronxville, NY 10708, 914/337-6668

The Garage Antiques Market, 111 W. 24th St. off 6th Ave. (open Saturdays)

NORTH CAROLINA CONSIGNMENTS

Metrolina Expo Flea Market, 7100 N. Statesville Road, Charlotte, NC 28269, 704/596-4643; 800/824-3770, www.metrolinaexpo.com

Consignment World, 9601 Independence Point Parkway, Matthews, NC 28105, 704/847-2620

Consignment World, 533 N. Polk St., Pineville, NC 28134, 704/889-8966

Transit Damaged Freight, 7917 Moore's Chapel Road, Charlotte, NC 28214, 704/392-8661 additional North Carolina locations: Kannapolis, Forest City, Bass, Durham, North Wilkesboro

OKLAHOMA CONSIGNMENTS

Consignment Treasures, 3525 S. Peoria, Tulsa, OK 74105, 918/742-8550

PENNSYLVANIA CONSIGNMENTS

Chestnut Hill Hospital Bargain, 8624 Germantown Avenue, Philadelphia, PA 19118, 215/248-1835

Jeanes Hospital Opportunity Shop, 7971 Oxford Avenue, Philadelphia, PA 19111, 215/742-0698

Medical Missions Thrift Shop, 8400 Pine Road, Philadelphia, PA 19111, 215/745-7930

Pennsylvania Hospital Bargain Shop, 719 Delancey Street, Philadelphia, PA 19106

TEXAS CONSIGNMENTS

Blue Bird Circle Resale Shop, 615 West Alabama, Houston, TX 77006, 713/528-0470

The Glassell School of Art, 5101 Montrose, Houston, TX 77006, 713/639-7500

The Guild Shop of St. John the Divine, 2009 Dunlavy, Houston, TX 77006, 713/528-5095, e-mail: guildshop@pcm.net

Houston Junior Forum Resale Shop, 1815 Rutland, Houston, TX 77008, 713/868-6970

Polly John's Consignment House, 2421 Sunset Blvd., Houston, TX 77005, 713/529-5999

Charity Guild of Catholic Women Resale Shop, 1203 Lovett, Houston, TX 77006, 713/529-0995,

Lewis & Maese Antiques, 2940 Ferndale, Houston, TX 77098, 713/942-7200

Habitat for Humanity Re-Store, 310 Comal, Ste. 101, Austin, TX 78702, 512/478-2165 AHREstore@aol.com; dbmackie@austin.rr.com

City-Wide Garage Sale, City Coliseum, 512 E. Riverside Dr., Austin, TX 78704, 512/441-7133

Last Call Neiman Marcus, 4115 S. Capitol of Texas Hwy, Austin, TX 78704, 512/447-0701

The Next to New Shop, 5308 Burnet Rd., Austin, TX 78756, 512/459-1288

Peacock Alley Outlet, 13720 Midway Rd., Dallas, TX 75244, 972/490-3998

Horchow Finale, 3046 Mockingbird Lane, Dallas, TX 75205, 214/750-0308 and 3400 Preston Rd., Plano, TX 75093, 972/519-5406

VIRGINIA CONSIGNMENT AND OUTLETS

Upscale Resale Qualtiy Consignments, 8100 Lee Hwy., Falls Church, VA 22042, 703/698-8100

Storehouse Furniture Clearance Center, 5898-A Leesburg Pike, Falls Church, VA 22042, 703/379-5327

Pier One Clearance Store, 3045 Columbia Pike, Arlington, VA 22204, 703/486-8164

WASHINGTON STATE CONSIGNMENTS

Children's Hospital Thrift Shop, 2026 Third Avenue, Seattle, WA 98121, 206/448-7609

Nationwide: Crate & Barrel outlets, 800/996-9960 or www.crateandbarrel.com

FABRICS

Calico Corners website (for store locations): www.calicocorners.com

ALABAMA FABRIC OUTLETS

B & B Outlet, 6th St., Hwy 231 S., Oneon, AL 35121, 205/274-2219, fax: 205/274-2288

ARKANSAS FABRIC OUTLETS

Cynthia East Fabrics, 1523 Rebsamen Park Rd., Little Rock, AR 72202, 501/663-0460

CALIFORNIA FABRIC OUTLETS

W.R. Fabrics, 963 Loma Santa Fe Drive, Solana Beach, CA 92075, 619/755-1175

Diamond Foam and Fabric, 611 S. La Brea, Los Angeles, CA 90036, 323/931-8148

D & S Discount Fabrics, 1000 15th St., 2nd Floor, San Francisco, CA 94103, 415/522-1098

Laura & Kiran Warehouse Sales, 542 Tenth Street, Berkeley, CA 94710, 510/647-1493; fax: 510/647-1490

Norman S. Bernie Co. Decorative Fabrics, 1135 N. Amphlett Blvd., San Mateo, CA 94401, 650/342-8586

Poppy Fabrics, 5151 Broadway, Oakland, CA 94611, 510/655-5151

S. Beressi Fabric Sales, 1504 Bryant St., 2nd Floor, San Francisco, CA 94103, 415/861-5004

The Silk Trading Company, 1616-A 16th St., San Francisco, CA 94122, 415/282-5574, www.siktrading.com

The Silk Trading Company, 360 La Brea Ave., Los Angeles, CA 90036, 213/954-9280

Wallstreet Factory Outlet, 2690 Harrison Street, San Francisco, CA 94110, 415/285-0870

Diamond Foam and Fabric, 611 S. La Brea, Los Angeles, CA 90036, 323/931-8148

Foam, 891 S. La Brea, Los Angeles, CA 90036, 323/931-3626

CONNECTICUT FABRIC OUTLETS

Home Fabric Mills, Inc. (mail order & stores) 882 South Main Street, P.O. Box 888, Cheshire, CT 06410, 203/272-3529; fax: 203/272-6686

Weathervane Hill Fabric Outlet Store, 85 A Water Street, South Norwalk, CT 06854, 203/852-6711

DELAWARE FABRIC OUTLETS

The Interior Alternative, 1325 Cooches Bridge Rd., Newark, DE 19713, 302/454-3232

New London Textiles, 200 Bellview Road, (P.O. Box 7768), Wilmington, DE 19714, 302/368-2571

SOURCES & RESOURCES

GEORGIA FABRIC OUTLETS
Forsythe Fabrics and Furniture, 1190 Foster
Place NW, Atlanta, GA 30354, 404/351-6050
Forsythe Fabrics Closeouts, 1168 Howell Mill
Rd. NW, Atlanta, GA 30318, 678/607-1064
Lewis & SharonTextile Co., 912 Huff Rd.,
Atlanta, GA 30318, 800/835-4833,
ILLINOIS FABRIC OUTLETS
BMI Home Decorating (mail order only),
6917 Catalpa Court, Spring Grove, IL 60081,
815/675-3703; fax: 815/675-0143
The Interior Alternative, 11800 Factory Shops
Blvd., Store #850, Huntley, IL 60142,
847/669-1651
KENTUCKY FABRIC OUTLETS
Hancock's of Paducah (mail order), 3841
Hinkleville Rd., Paducah, KY 42001, 800/834-
8723; fax: 502/442-2164
e-mail: DsingBear@aol.com;
website: www.fabric-world.com
MASSACHUSETTS FABRIC OUTLETS
Harmony Supply, Inc. (mail order & store
location), P.O. Box 313, 18 High St., Medford,
MA 02155, 781/395-2600; fax: 781/396-8218
The Fabric Center, Inc. (mail order only),
485 Electric Avenue, Fitchburg, MA 01420,
508/343-4402; fax: 508/343-8139
MINNESOTA FABRIC OUTLETS
Grand Remnants, 1136 Grand Avenue, St. Paul,
MN 55105, 651/221-0221
S.R. Harris Fabric Outlet, 8865 Zealand Ave. N,
Brooklyn Park, MN 55445, 612/424-3500
Designer Home Fabrics, 5018 France Ave. S,
Edina, MN 55410, 612/925-0562
Mill End Textiles, Warehouse Store, 10100
Crosstown Circle, Eden Prairie, MN 55344,
612/941-5350
Fabrics N Homes Ltd., 13000 Aldrich Ave. S,
Burnsville, MN 55306, 612/894-4993
NEW JERSEY FABRIC SHOPS
Marlene's Decorator Fabrics (mail order only),
301 Beech Street, Hackensack, NJ 07601,
201/843-0844
NEW YORK FABRIC OUTLETS
Richard's, 1390 Lexington Avenue, New York,
NY 10128, 212/831-9000
NORTH CAROLINA FABRIC OUTLETS
Hang-It-Now Wallpaper Stores (mail order &

store location), 304 Trindale Road, Archdale,
NC 27263, 800/325-9494; fax: 910/431-0449
PENNSYLVANIA FABRIC OUTLETS
Benington's (mail order catalog & seven retail
locations in PA & VA), 1271 Manheim Pike,
Lancaster, PA 17601, 800/252-5060;
fax: 717/299-4889; website: www.beni.com
SOUTH CAROLINA
Forest Lake Fabric, 4865 Forest Drive, Columbia,
SC 29206, 803/782-5916
TEXAS FABRIC SHOPS
Leggett's, 2600 Capitol, Houston, TX 77003,
713/222-2471
Check It Out. 214 South Rogers, Waxahachie,
TX 75165, 972/938-2403
Durham Trading & Design Company,
1009 W. 6th, Austin, TX 78703, 512/476-1216

OTHER SOURCES

MONTREAL, CANADA, SHOPS
Les Village des Antiquaires, 1708 Notre Dame
Ouest, Montreal, Canada, 514/931-5121
Passé & Présent, 320 rue St-Paul Ouest,
Montreal, QC H2Y 2A3, Canada, 514/499-0062;
fax: 514/499-3056, http://pages.infinit.net/passepr,
e-mail: elleiram@caramail.com
Antiquité Décoration Art, 1838 rue Notre-Dame
Ouest, Montreal, QC H3J 1M5, 514/937-2440
DMC Antiquities, 1874 Rue Notre-Dame Ouest,
Montreal, QC H3J 1M6, Canada, 514/931-6722
Pierre St. Jacques Antiquaire, 2507 Notre-Dame
Ouest, Montreal, QC H3J 1N6, 514/933-9293
Fleur de juin Fleuriste, 2507 Notre-Dame Ouest,
Montreal, QC H3J 1N6, Canada, 514/933-2520
Lucie Favreau, 1904 Notre-Dame Ouest,
Montreal, QC H3J 1M6, Canada, 514/989-5117;
fax: 514/989-1552
Ambiance Antiquités and Antiques, 1612 Ouest
Notre Dame W., Montreal, QC H3J 1M1, 514/939-
8813
Antiquités Le Design, 1604 Nortre-Dame Ouest,
Montreal, QC H3J 1M1, Canada, 514/939-1594;
fax: 514/939-1484
L'Apostrophe, 2617 Rue Notre Dame Ouest,
Montreal, QC H3J 1N9, Canada, 514/933-3866
CATALOGS AND RETAIL LOCATIONS:
Ballard Designs, 800/367-2810

Horchow Home, 800/456-7000
The Home Depot, 800/553-3199
Kmart, 800/551-7821
Pier One Imports, 800/447-4371
Crate & Barrel, 800/996-9960
Pottery Barn, 800/922-9934, 800/922-5507
Restoration Hardware, 800/762-1005
Target Stores, 800/800-8800
IKEA, 800/434-4532, www.ikea.com
Lowe's, 336/658-7100

REAL LIFE SOURCES

CAREFREE ON THE COAST
Pages 12-25: design: Jeffrey Alan Marks,
1040 W. Muirland Drive, La Jolla, CA 92037,
858/459-9192; 7906 Hillside Ave., Los Angeles,
CA 90048; 323/207-2222; regional editor: Andrea
Caughey, San Diego; photography, Bill Holt,
Larkspur, CA; Renovation: Rancho Pacific
Builders, 619/253-5069.
Dining room: dining table: JAM Designs; roman
shades: JAM Designs, constructed by Draperies
by Picazo; venetian plaster wall finish: Mark
Chavis of Texture; painting: Lendrum Fine Art:
858/549-3989.
Fireplace area: art on mantle: Leslie Saris; side
chair fabric: Bennison Fabric; andiron: Downtown,
Los Angeles; loveseat: JAM Designs, Joseph
Noble Fabric; pillow on loveseat: Nancy Corzine.
Window area: sectional sofa: JAM Designs;
pillows: Fortuny Fabric; sisal: Amari Flooring;
mirrors: Lendrum Fine Arts; pedestal table: City
Antiques, Los Angeles: 323/658-6354;.
Guest bedroom: roman shades: Draperies by
Picazo; fabric: Chelsea Textiles.
Master bedroom: headboard: JAM Designs; fabric:
Great Plains Fabric; bedskirt: Great Plains Fabric;
cylinder lamp with paper shade: Divan Studios:
858/551-2662
LIVING WITH LATIN HERITAGE
Pages 26-37: Design: Aurora Barcenas,
fax: 713/629-6408; regional editor: Joetta
Moulden; Houston, TX; photography: Jenifer
Jordan, Waxahatchie, TX; Oriental rugs: Texas
Oriental Rugs, Houston, custom-made furniture
(loggia): David Solano; Houston; major paintings—
living room over mantel: Franco Penalba; breakfast

dining area: Hugo Palma Ibarra.

BABY MAKES THREE

Pages: 38-47: regional editor: Nancy Ingram, Tulsa, OK; photography: Jenifer Jordan; slipcovers, draperies, pillows, soft fabrications: Judy Elkhoury Fabrications: 918/712-2881; fabric for nursery: Kinsho (red) from Designers' Guild (order through an interior designer); brass letters and other accessories: T.A. Lorton, Tulsa, 918/743-1600; accessories: Elements, Tulsa, 918/587-8899.

OPPOSITES ATTRACT:

Pages 48-59: architect: Alan Rudy; structural engineer: Rajenda Sahai; design consulting: Marion Philpotts, ASID, Your Space, San Francisco, CA , 415/357-9800; regional editor: Carla Howard, San Francisco; photography: Bill Holt, Larkspur, CA; custom built-in and custom bedside tables: Philip Agee, Muleland, San Francisco, CA; 415/626-4276; Italian-style colored plasterwork: Chris Stefano, CSV, San Francisco; 415/206-0235; drapery fabrication: Tom Malatesta, Malatesta and Company, San Francisco; 415/558-8840; custom velvet by Sherrie Brody, through the designer or in Tesuque, NM, 505/986-9213; slipcovers: custom-made slipcovers by Rogelio: 415/386-0805; Slips, San Francisco, 415/362-5652; leather furniture in living room and bedroom, dining room table, benches in front of windows in living room (stainless steel and reclaimed wood): Zonal, San Francisco, 415/563-2220; fabric on living room window seat: The Silk Trading Co., 415/282-5574; fireplace mantel tile and kitchen backsplash tile: Ann Sacks Tile & Stone, 415/252-5889; window treatments in the dining area: Castec shades: 800/828-2500; The Roman Shade Co., 415/621-2777; Moroccan tables: Wroolie & Co., 415/863-8815; Chinese lanterns in kitchen area: Nest: 415/292-6199; bedside lamps in master bedroom: Aria, 415/433-0219.

Deborah Bishop also suggests the following San Francisco sources for furniture and accessories: Aria, 415/433-0219; Alabaster, 415/558-0482, and deVera. She has found many of her treasures at the Chelsea Flea Market in New York City and the Sausalito and Alemany Markets in San Francisco.

FILLING THE EMPTY NEST:

Pages 60-71: Design: Carolyn Carroll, Little Rock, AR; regional editor: Dianne Carroll, Dallas, Texas; photography: Jenifer Jordan; antiquities, furnishings and accessory sources: Pslugrads, Little Rock, Antiquarius, Little Rock, Marshall Clements, Little Rock.

THE FAMILY PROJECT:

Pages 72-83: Design and decorative painting by Gwen Hauser, St. Paul, MN, 651/698-5122; regional editor: Tangi Schaapveld; photography: Susan Gilmore, Minneapolis, MN.

GLAMOUR IN THE CITY:

Pages 84-85: Regional editor: Heather Lobdell, Chevy Chase, MD; photography: D. Randolph Foulds; kitchen design: Jan Gilmore; kitchen: painting next to white sofa: LaShun Beal; Tina's Gallery, North Potomac, MD, 301/-320-4611; in window above wine refrigerator: Shona stone sculpture (Zimbabwe), Creative Artisans, Odenton, MD, 301/912-3992; televison cabinet: Bali reproduction by Crate and Barrel; pillows: Crate and Barrel; kitchen table from Northern Thailand: SUMA Imports, San Francisco, CA; dining room: rug: Terra Cognita, Bethesda, MD, 301/907-3055; chargers, plates, table linens: Ancient Rhythms, Bethesda: 301/652-2669; painting by Anita Philyaw, 202/244-0421; living room: painting on easel: Marvin Posey, Tina's Gallery; painting over fireplace: Elizabeth Martineau, Tina's Gallery; office: photograph over daybed: Phil Borges, The Studio Gallery, San Diego, CA, 888-294-9880; wood carving: Ancient Rhythms, Bethesda; MD; ottoman: Terra Cognita.

NEWLY WED BLISS:

Pages 96-105: Design and color consulting: Donna L. Wendt, Saratoga, NY; stylist: Heather Lobdell; photography: Gordon Beall, Chevy Chase, MD; paint: courtesy of Benjamin Moore & Co.: 800/826-2623; rugs in kitchen, family room, and living room, hardware for kitchen cabinets and living room built-in, kitchen sink, Lowe's: 336-658-7100; www.lowes.com; countertop installation: Mark Wagner, The Cabinet Shop, Clifton Park, NY, 518/383-0962; dining area Roman shade: Val Papero, The Shade Place; slipcover: Jean Fleming.

LIVING WITH THE EXOTIC:

Pages 106-117: Regional editor: Elle Roper, Atlanta, GA; photography: Emily Minton, Atlanta, GA; console table and coffee tables in living room and office/guest room are from The Minton-Corley Collection, based in Fort Worth, TX, 817/332-8993. Country French armoire and dining table are antiques from Minton-Corley; armoire and dining table are from Joseph Minton Antiques, Dallas; candelabra in the living room is by Jan Barboglio, Dallas, TX. Her work is sold through Neiman-Marcus, 800-825-8000.

MOVING TO THE BURBS:

Pages 118-129: Regional editor: Heather Lobdell; photograpahy: Gordon Beall; design: Patrick Sutton, Alexandria, VA, 703/549-5739; website: www.suttondesign.com; custom built-ins in library: D. Christian Thompson, Clifton, VA., 703/705-9505; paint: courtesy of Benjamin Moore & Co: 800/826-2623; leather chairs, ottoman, console table, drink table, lamps, white vase in library: Restoration Hardware, 800/762-1005; prints in library: Prints & Photographs Reading Room, Library of Congress, 202/707-6394 or http://lcweb.lc.govt; chairs in dining room: Pottery Barn, 800/922-9934; custom kitchen tile: Pandemonium, Key West, FL; custom lineoleum: Carpet One of Alexandria, 703/370-0000; rug in dining room: Odegard Carpets, 202/484-5888; linens in master bedroom: Palais Royal, Alexandria, VA, 703/549-6660. For an additional source of quality American-history-based photography prints, the Bogers also suggest the John F. Kennedy Library in Boston, 617/929-4500.

ADDITIONAL PHOTO CREDITS

Page 137: (left) photography: Gordon Beall.
Page 139: (left) project design: Deborah Hastings, Birmingham, AL; photography: Emily Minton.
Page 142: (left) project design/styling: Elizabeth Donner; photography: Emily Minton.
Page 150: Design: Cecilia Bayer-Thayer; The Homestead, Fredricksburg, Texas; regional editor: Mary Baskin; photography: Jenifer Jordan.
Page 153: (left) photography: Gordon Beall; (right) design: Deborah Hastings; photography: Emily Minton.
Page 154: (left) project design: Deborah Hastings; photography: Emily Minton.

INDEX